NAME
ANIMAL PLACE THING

An inspiring fable about hope,
positivity, and living your best life

Lux Narayan

www.NPAT.life

Notion Press

First Published by Notion Press 2021
No. 8, 3rd Cross Street, CIT Colony, Mylapore,
Chennai, Tamil Nadu – 600004, India

ISBN
Paperback: 978-1-63669-576-1
Hardcover: 978-1-63781-663-9
EBook: 978-1-63669-577-8

www.NPAT.life

Dedication

To my parents, sons, family, friends, and teachers.
And especially to my wife, Tina,
for never saying, "Only an idiot would do that."

"A human being should be able to change a diaper, plan an invasion, butcher a hog, conn a ship, design a building, write a sonnet, balance accounts, build a wall, set a bone, comfort the dying, take orders, give orders, cooperate, act alone, solve equations, analyze a new problem, pitch manure, program a computer, cook a tasty meal, fight efficiently, and die gallantly. Specialization is for insects (and I will add doctors)."

– Robert Heinlein

Contents

"There is nothing better than a friend, unless it is a friend with chocolate."

— *Linda Grayson*

CHAPTER 1

A Party

W hen's the best time to have a breakdown? Perhaps, never?

Were someone to rank the worst times to have one, six hours before your 50th birthday might top that list.

John was having precisely that. A breakdown of the existential kind. At Lincoln Park, New Jersey, at the Sunset Pub & Grill. The restaurant, a favorite among aviators, was right next to the general aviation airport runway. The watering-hole lived up to its reputation as a beautiful place to watch the sunset while painting the sky with a palette that changed colors with the seasons. One could also celebrate feats of engineering and human ingenuity in the small planes and helicopters that took off and landed as they practiced their pattern work.

It was also a great place to eat and catch up with old friends, which was what we were doing. John, Raj, Mona, and me.

We were a close-knit group of four friends who had stayed in regular touch ever since we'd graduated from college. We tried to meet at least once every two years, usually at one of our homes. When work or life took us to each others' cities, we had an open invitation to a spare bed of some flavor. A great meal, a stiff drink, and old-world camaraderie were always guaranteed. We shared experiences and stories as we moved jobs and careers across countries and continents. We traded joys and sorrows as we dated, got married, had children, cared for, and sometimes lost parents, grew in our careers and waistlines, and settled into our respective suburban existences across the world.

This time, our excuse for catching up was John's 50th birthday, which we were hoping to ring in at midnight. In exactly six hours and twenty minutes.

As we suspected, and later learned, a birthday was the very last thing on John's mind. John's wife initially wanted to have a large party calling a few dozen of their friends, many of whom were ours too, but John would have none of that. A few months earlier, John had undergone angioplasty for a block in his heart. It was in his left descending artery—one that doctors cruelly called 'the widowmaker.' John was reasonably fit, and so, we were all surprised. The doctors attributed it to stress and its unhealthy companions.

As far as we were all concerned, his 50th was a huge reason to celebrate as he found the arterial block in time, addressed it, and lived to see fifty in reasonably good health. After much convincing by his wife and us, John reluctantly agreed to a quieter event—catching up with just the three of us. We should have guessed then that something else was bothering him. There was a slow but rapidly increasing hum of discontent.

"Kai, this is a lovely place," John said, looking at me and pointing in the general direction of the sounds of banter around us. "But, is this even a reason to celebrate? I mean, if you think about it, all that's happened is that the Earth has gone around the Sun fifty times since I was born. That's it. There's nothing else to it."

And as if to illustrate his point, John walked around the three of us at our outdoor table with his half-finished glass of Guinness in hand, distracting our attention from a Piper Archer that had made a textbook perfect landing on Runway 19.

"And why fifty? Why this obsession with multiples of five and ten? Why not seven? We should have celebrated my forty-ninth birthday before I went into the hospital. And next, my fifty-sixth. And then..."

Raj cut him off just as John's voice was embarking upon higher octaves.

"All right. We now know that you remember your multiplication tables. It's the least we'd expect from a successful investment banker—the ability to count. Why tens? There are many reasons for adopting the decimal system, starting with the number of fingers we have. Or as they're often known, digits..."

"There he goes on another tangent," Mona groaned.

Raj, a Physics professor at Oxford, had a reputation for knowing something about everything, but this was certainly not the right time or occasion for a discourse on the evolution of number systems. Raj also had a bad reputation as far as his sense of timing was concerned. He almost seemed oblivious to the context of things. Knowing him as well as we did, we accepted that it was his price for brilliance.

"Raj, let's discuss numbers another time?" Mona implored. "For now, a couple of things. First, John, could you please sit? Between those planes taking off and landing, my almost perfect margarita, and your impersonation of planet Earth orbiting the Sun, I'm starting to feel like I'm on a theme-park ride. And second, we thought this is what you wanted and finally agreed to? A tetra-celebration."

Over the years, the four of us had gotten used to prefixing our catch-ups with the word *Tetra*. Tetra-vacations, tetra-dinners, tetra-anything were all the subject lines of emails exchanged. Even our WhatsApp group was called Tetra. It was our unique word from the name of a short-lived rock band we'd formed at college. We were high on ambition but short on talent.

"Yeah," I chimed in. "What's up? Something's eating you. And knowing you as well as we do, it appears it's been eating you for a while now?"

John (thankfully) sat down again, took a quick breath, and let out a prolonged sigh. One of those sighs that sound like someone has the weight of the world on their shoulders and hopes they can breathe it away or into submission.

"You're right," he said. "This has been bouncing around in my head for a while now."

"What has?" the three of us asked with our eyes.

"My life," John continued. "Of late, I seem to be questioning everything. I'm pretty sure that when we were at college if you'd asked me what I wanted, this is not what I would have described."

"This?" Raj asked.

"Yeah. This. A life that feels like a personalized version of the script for Groundhog Day—doing the same thing day after day after day after day."

Mona, feeling another Earth impersonation coming from John, cut him off.

"John, that's pretty strange coming from you. If you ask anyone who knows you, they'd say you have everything—a great life, a loving family, an upward career, talented and grounded kids who are doing well at college. Anyone would be envious. And hey, you even have a 50th birthday celebration with all this," she said as she stretched her hands to include the landscape around us. "You're lucky that you are younger than the three of us. Remember how it was when each of us turned fifty? We celebrated over tetra-Zoom calls. We had no other option."

"Oh yeah," Raj added. "Don't remind us about 2020. The year of the rat that ended up becoming the year of the virus. Don't we remember it all too well even though it was three years ago?"

"Yeah, yeah, yeah," John said. "I know. And I don't mean to sound ungrateful for all that. I know I'm fortunate. Very fortunate. For my family. For my career. For friends like you. For not celebrating my 50th in front of a webcam. I know I am blessed. I do. But something's missing. The crazy thing is that I don't even know what it is. It feels like a void—an emptiness that has been getting louder in my gut for some time now. The best way I can put it is that it's a feeling that I should be doing more. More... More stuff, I guess."

"Stuff?" I asked, confused.

"Yeah, stuff," he continued. "I don't know what it is, but I know there is something else out there that I ought to be doing. I can feel it in my bones. And it's been eating me. Eating me on a regular schedule, each time I get my pay-check, and am reminded that I'm a corporate slave who has agreed to pay for his wages with his health and dreams. Turning fifty brought it up to the surface and…"

John trailed off before abruptly standing and declaring, "Sorry, but I need some air."

He walked away from the restaurant and toward the taxiway where a couple of planes were doing their run-ups.

"Do you think he's OK?" Mona asked, concerned.

"I hope so," I answered, looking towards Raj.

Raj was silent. He was watching John walk on to one of the taxiways.

John was getting precariously close to a King Air that was also doing a run-up about two-hundred feet away. John had his hands akimbo and was looking up at the sky. He seemed oblivious to all the action around him.

A lineman came running out of a nearby hangar in less than a minute, animatedly waving his hands. While John couldn't hear his words over the din of the planes doing their pre-flight checks, the message was clear. From the lineman's gestures and raised voice, we gathered that John was asked to leave and head back to the restaurant.

Others at the Sunset Pub had interrupted their libations to see what the commotion was about.

John stepped off the taxiway and onto the adjoining grass strip sandwiched between the restaurant and the airport. He ambled aimlessly for a bit like a child sulking after being scolded. Finally, and to our collective relief, he walked back towards us.

A few other patrons' amused expressions followed John as he came back and sheepishly seated himself in his chair. We'd decided not to ask him anything about his reckless stroll.

"A rouble for your thoughts," I said, referring to an inside joke we had in college. It was about Russian hyperinflation during the Cold War and how some of our thoughts and ideas were worth little.

John's slight smile indicated that he caught the reference.

"Nothing much," he answered. "I'm thinking about something I'd last thought of when I was in the hospital—what my obituary would say. JOHN. Great husband, awesome dad, consummate family man. A good friend. And a banker par excellence. Wow. The weekend classifieds sound more interesting."

As if to echo John's mood, the sun moved behind a cloud at the same time that a silver-blue Mooney turned from base to final following a Cirrus that had entered the landing flare.

"Whoa," Raj said as he mock-punched John on his arm. "Why are we even discussing obituaries five and a half hours before your birthday? And by the way, count yourself lucky in that department as well. I learned somewhere that John is the most prolific name among obituaries featured in the New York Times. So, you have an edge for being featured in the Times after you die," he laughed, trying to lighten up the mood with his morbid sense of humor. We were accustomed to it.

John managed another weak smile. "OK. Add that then to that long list of things that I'm grateful for."

"If I'm honest, and please believe me when I say that this is not fake empathy," Raj continued, after a thoughtful pause, "I think I can relate to what you're feeling, John. I've felt it myself. It felt discordant but less so now after hearing you talk about it."

I was the first to speak after an awkward silence, "Seriously, professor? You?"

Many of us had always called him professor back in college, but the moniker recently gained new respectability and notoriety after the runaway success of the Spanish series *La Casa de Papel* aka *Money Heist* on Netflix. It was also a testament to the fact that great stories transcend languages, cultures, and boundaries.

"You're at Oxford," I continued. "The hallowed seat of learning. Young and curious minds hang on to your every word, and you are sought out for your cutting-edge research and scintillating talks. And let's not even go into how you punched way above your weight when you got married. You? You're telling us that you feel this way? C'mon. Get real."

I regretted my words the moment I said them. Raj's marriage had recently ended in an amicable but unhappy divorce. I was still good friends with his ex-wife, who I continued to believe was an amazing person.

"Yeah, I do. I can't help it," Raj snapped, choosing to ignore my flippant comment about his marriage. "Remember when we were young? I played the guitar then. I haven't touched it in decades, but one of my favorite songs was "Time" by Pink Floyd. Unfortunately, one line from that song often plays in my head these days."

"Let me guess," John interrupted, "it's the one that ends with thinking you had more to say?"

John and Raj began an off-key rendition of disconnected verses of the song when I interrupted them.

"Hey. Hey. Hey. I thought I was at a tetra-hangout, not Pessimists Anonymous," I said, hoping to lighten the mood and simultaneously end the cacophony.

"That's very easy for you to say," Mona snapped, raising her voice.

"Whoa. Where did that come from?"

Mona had been silent for some time, but it was evident that John and Raj's mood was contagious and spreading fast. All my friends seemed to be nurturing some form of existential angst.

"Yeah. Sure, you can easily say that," she continued. "I can relate to what these guys are saying. I feel it too. I first felt it three years ago when I took that break from work, and it came back in full force last year when we became empty-nesters. I thought that a sense of purpose had been wrenched away from me when the kids left for college."

Inside my head, I was shaking with disbelief. Sought after in speaking and conference circuits, and as a consultant, Mona was once considered a marketing guru of sorts. In a career that crossed countries, categories, brands, and products, she had carved out a stellar reputation for herself. In recent years, some family circumstances had forced her to take a break from her illustrious career. Always the most pragmatic among the four of us, I'd imagined everything in her life was neatly laid out. Like the dinner table at her house when we met there a few years ago with a knife and fork assigned for each course even if it was wasted on folks like us.

I was seemingly wrong about Mona. I saw a side to my friends that I'd been oblivious to so far.

"So, yeah. It's easy for you to say that" repeated Mona, interrupting my thoughts and reiterating her point if I hadn't registered it the first time around.

"Wait. What exactly do you mean?" I asked again.

"I can't imagine you feel the way we do. Or even being able to understand it or relate to it," she continued.

"Yeah, you seem to be doing something new every time," added Raj. "When you came to London on work last year, I almost got a headache listening to everything that you were up to."

"A new hobby. A new idea. A new sport. A new something all the time," said John, jumping into the fray of what, to anyone eavesdropping on our conversation, would have sounded like the three of them ganging up on me.

John continued, "You seem to be blessed with more than the twenty-four hours the rest of us got. Nowadays, you always seem… how do I put it? Happy."

"And crazy curious," Mona added, completing the circle of accusations.

I raised my hands in surrender. "All right, all right. Easy there. If it's happiness you're accusing me of, then I'm guilty as charged. I'm not going to deny it. I am indeed happy. And yes, I'm doing a lot of stuff, and I'm glad for it. Even if it often feels like I'm biting off more than I can chew. Life has been fuller since the pandemic. This happier, more curious me is my new normal, I guess. It's been a while, so I don't even realize how much I've changed. For the better, I'd like to think."

"Absolutely. So, tell us what changed?" John asked, echoing the curious expression in Raj and Mona's eyes. "I know it wasn't the relief from the lockdowns ending.

That happened to us all. We all went through that pressure valve being finally released."

"Funny you said that," I said with a wistful smile.

"Said what?"

"About the lockdown ending. That's almost exactly when my life changed. I call the period before that as BC—Before Coronavirus."

They laughed. It was the first honest laugh I'd heard from my dear friends in the last thirty minutes.

"What's AD, then? After Disease? But seriously," Mona asked, "What gives? You're speaking in riddles now. What happened to you since the pandemic?"

"Permit me one more riddle, and then, I promise I'll explain," I said while pulling out my phone and opening my Photos app. "They say a picture is worth a thousand words. This picture here captures my current plan for what I'm up to and what I plan to do. This. Single. Picture."

I held the phone at the center of the table and they all leaned in to take a closer look as if it were the answer to life, the universe, and everything.

"It looks like something my kids would have drawn on a bad art day," Mona added. Her children were adults, but she still called them kids.

"Yeah, when they were five," Raj chuckled.

"It's like a stick figure of a person," John said. "With text scrawled at various places—text that I can't even read, which isn't surprising, given your handwriting. You should have been a doctor, Kai."

Laughing, I took my phone back. "Now that you've critiqued my artistic abilities let me tell you the story behind this picture. Two years ago, after the pandemic was over, I felt something that I now remember to have been like what you all described. It came from a different place, though. It's what happened after, and the amazing people I met and learned from that remarkably changed my perspective on life—a fuller life. It changed me at my core. So much so, I don't even realize now that I have changed."

"Well, speaking of your core, you're looking fitter and younger for one," said Mona.

"And glowing," added John, as my friends embarrassed me with their platitudes.

"Out with it," Raj said, mock-raising his voice and changing his intonation to imitate a Shakespearean play ostensibly. "Pray, tell us. What is this secret that thou hast discovered?"

We all laughed together. For the second time in five minutes. Not bad. Almost on cue, the sun came out from behind the clouds where it had been hiding. The sky looked beautiful, and the light was picture perfect. It was what photographers referred to as the golden hour.

"All right," I said. "But you asked for it, and I must warn you that this will take some time. Are you folks sure you want to do this today? On your 50th, John?"

"What better day for it, old chap?" John said, with his own rendition of an English voice that sounded like a poorly defined character from a P.G. Wodehouse novel.

He continued, "It's a great time for self-reflection and learning. I assume you learned something that you're going to share with us before supper. Some instant magic formula, perhaps? I could certainly use one."

"I agree," I said. "It's a great time for reflection and making change happen. Not because it's your 50th but because it's now. That's the first thing I learned—that there is no auspicious time. Now is the best time for almost everything. It's like that expression about the best time to plant a tree being several years ago. The second-best time is now."

John nodded as I continued, "And second, there is no instant magic formula, I'm afraid. There are some magical processes, but there's no instant formula. You will have to do the hard but enjoyable work. It also depends on what you count as work, of course. I can only say that, as you all observed and kindly mentioned, I've changed for the better. My life does feel full. Like a pot that's constantly boiling over."

"Now, that reminds me of your cooking soon after we graduated from college," teased Mona.

I laughed, "Many a kitchen disaster from the past springs to mind. It's gotten better over the years, as you will hopefully agree. OK, you folks asked for it. Let's refill our drinks first, and then I'll tell you some stories. Funnily enough, it all started two years ago on an evening when I was meeting some friends like we're doing right now."

* * *

"Under certain circumstances, profanity provides a relief denied even to prayer."

— Mark Twain

CHAPTER 2

A Pandemic

*T*wo years ago…

We got our first flavor of that evening's plans when Gina changed our WhatsApp group's name to *Mask Burning Party*.

Besides Gina and me, our 'neighborhood group' included Neil, who was married to Gina, Jasmine, and Joe, who I'd known for the longest time.

I was curious as I stared at the very helpful *"Gina is typing…"* message on my phone. Finally, my screen came alive with a new chat blurb. Her message said:

Hey, you all. Coming Saturday. Drinks & BBQ at our place. Just BYOM. That's short for Bring Your Old Mask. For burning. Bloody f***ing time.

Knowing Gina, I assumed that a combination of the bra-burning movement and her recent fascination with the culture and evolution of burning-man had inspired this. Being accustomed to her penchant for symbolism and drama, I wasn't surprised. And why not, indeed, considering everything that had happened these past many months. Why not a mask burning party? It was *Bloody f***ing time.*

We were five good friends meeting up in 2021 when the pandemic that had washed out most of 2020 in more ways than one was on its very last legs.

We'd been mute witnesses to a year when billions of people learned more about charts, graphs, and statistics than they had in their entire lives before that. Unfortunately, the charts, graphs, and statistics were all about losing jobs, getting sick, or dying.

The prevailing sense of 'dystopia,' a word that had only recently entered the popular lexicon, was finally fading. The vaccine was now a proven reality with a globally believable, implementable, and visible timeline.

It had been first administered to high-risk populations and front-line workers, quite deservedly. It was only a matter of time before everyone else got it. A daily ticker celebrated the growing percentage of the world population who were vaccinated. That particular day's number was "79%." That was over six billion Earthlings, all in all. Typically administered in two doses, the volume of vaccine dispensed so far was what a hundred oil tanker trucks might carry. If only it were as easy as transporting oil.

Countries across the globe, inward-looking and jingoistic at first, finally collaborated to create a global supply chain of epic proportions. For the first time, a product would have a worldwide market of 7.8 billion people. Hopefully, it was also the last time.

The only other thing that the entire human race had consumed was "air." Even clean water, unfortunately, doesn't qualify as a global consumable.

It was a reason to celebrate. An end to the pandemic was finally near.

Many of the restrictions that had, in recent months, redefined our routines and daily lives had partially been lifted. We could now move past the lens of assuming that everyone else was a potential carrier. It was a lens that forced us to regard one another with a flavor of suspicion that was enforced, and fortunately, for most of us, never felt normal. Or human.

At Gina and Neil's lovely home, we first hugged as we'd last done many moons ago. It felt like an eternity, and we all realized how much of a sensory experience 'touch' is and its importance in, quite literally, connecting the human race. 'Touch' was a constrained experience in the recent past, one best executed from behind the safety of gloved hands.

Except for Joe. He was never a hugger, and the pandemic normalized that. He also declined a drink when Gina offered one.

"What? Have you become a teetotaler since we last met?" Gina asked.

"No such thing," Joe laughed. "I'm on call today."

"On-call?" Neil asked, surprised.

"Yeah, don't tell us you earned a medical degree during the lockdown?" I added.

"Ha. No way, Kai," Joe laughed. He always had a comfortable and spontaneous laugh. "Infectious," one would have said before that became a scary word.

"I'll tell you everything about it," he continued, "but I'll save it for when Jasmine gets here. I'm sure she'll ask me again. I'll give you a hint though—it has something to do with Gina's theme for today."

"Speak of the devil," Neil interrupted, as Jasmine's beacon of a car, an egg-yolk yellow Nissan convertible, pulled into their driveway.

"Ah, finally. And about time. The yellow submarine surfaces," Gina shouted out as a fitter, and younger-looking Jasmine in a flowery dress made her way, arms outstretched, towards the four of us. She radiated good health and positivity.

Jasmine hugged Gina, Neil, and me, and paused, doing a stop-start dance of sorts with Joe, till he complied. "Well, what the heck. Bring it in. Only for today." We all laughed and joined in what looked like a pre-match huddle a sports team would make.

We were all grateful to be alive, healthy, and together again.

"All right. First things first," Gina said, breaking up our huddle and assuming the voice of a circus ringmaster. "I hope you all brought your old masks?" The four of us obediently nodded as we pulled them out of our respective pockets.

"OK, stretch them out and hold them up high above your heads with your left hand."

We all played along. We were our own little barmy-army.

"Now, salute your mask with your right hand. *SAAAAAA-LUTE*. And finally, throw it with gratitude into the fire pit as a symbolic way of returning its carbon and other constituent elements to the Earth."

"How does one throw something with gratitude, anyway?" Jasmine asked no one in particular.

"Do it, or you're not getting any food tonight," Gina threatened with a smile.

If you hadn't guessed, Gina was also into conservation. And yes, she believed that a bit of drama never hurt anyone. But I must admit, burning that mask was cathartic even for a rationalist like me.

Ceremonies complete, and drinks in hand, we all gathered around the barbeque. Less than six feet apart. Like old times.

"Joe was waiting for you to arrive to tell us why he's on call," Neil informed Jasmine.

"What, you're a doctor now?" she asked, confused.

"I had the same question," I laughed. "Joe's not answered us yet."

Joe had a remarkable ability to rapidly learn anything he set his mind to. He and I knew each other from high school, and his ability to absorb things while seemingly paying scant attention was the envy of all. It was also a minor irritant to our teachers, some of whom believed that hard work needed to be visibly hard.

So, we were only half-joking when we asked him if he was now a doctor. With Joe, it was within the realm of possibility.

It turns out he was. Well, almost.

"Ha, no," Joe repeated. "But, you're close. I'm an EMT. And, I'm on call every alternate Saturday, today being one such day. So, close but no cigar."

"So, what's an EMT?" I asked.

"It stands for Emergency Medical Technician. I'm an EMT with our town's volunteer ambulance service. When you call 911, we're one of the places they'd contact in turn. We often get on the scene first to provide emergency medical assistance—stuff like CPR. We're usually the first people on the scene at local accidents too. And I've unfortunately seen some bad ones."

"Wow," Neil said, as did the looks of admiration in all our eyes. "You're sure to be a hit at parties. Designated driver and first aid provider rolled into one. Gina, let's take him along everywhere we're invited?"

We all laughed. We had so many questions, all at the same time.

"Why an EMT?"

"When did all this happen?"

"You did this during the lockdown? How?"

"You don't even like to hug. How're you going to do CPR?"

"Whoa. Whoa. One at a time, folks. Take a ticket and stand in line. OK, let me try and answer all that. Let's start with the why. It all started sometime around the third week of the lockdown. I was catching up with my cousin over a Facetime call."

"The cousin who's a doc in London?" I asked.

"Yup, same guy. He asked me how my day was and why I was looking rather stressed. I told him that I'd learned that our consulting firm had lost a pitch we'd recently made. Winning that pitch was key. It was critical for business, team morale, and me. Given the chemistry we felt between the prospect's team and ours during the pitch, we were blind-sided. We had been so confident that we'd win. Short of popping open the champagne, we had taken victory for granted."

We were all listening with rapt attention as Joe continued, "I rambled on and on, and only after doing so for a few minutes, I realized that I hadn't asked my cousin how his day was. So, out of a sense of politeness, I finally did. He told me that it was like any other day. He had a patient die on him during a particularly complicated surgery. The odds were fifty-fifty, but his team was confident of success. All in a regular day's work, he added."

"It hit me like a freak hailstorm in the middle of summer," Joe continued.

"I realized that we all have such different definitions of what is stressful and what the consequences of failure are. No job can match its negative consequences to that of the loss of life. After hearing about his day, losing that pitch seemed rather insignificant."

He added, "I'm not saying that the medical profession is the only one that matters. I'm only sharing that I began to introspect a lot more. The pandemic and the acute shortage of frontline workers strongly influenced me. All my fancy management models and their inapplicability made me feel misplaced. I felt I was in a tuxedo at a pool party."

He paused to let that image sink in and grab a sip of his seltzer before continuing, "I was sharing these thoughts with a client, Cora. She opened my eyes to the fact that in a few months, and over two-hundred hours of work, I could become a certified EMT. She added that this was even possible during the lockdown as hybrid online and offline courses were available. So, that week, without over-thinking, I signed up. A few months, two-hundred hours, and an exam later, here I am."

You could have cut the silence with a knife.

"Respect, Joe," I said, echoing what was in all our hearts and minds. I even raised my hands in a salute like Gina had just made us do.

"OK, enough about me," said Joe, uncomfortable at being the center of attention. "Let's talk about something else. Like, how we all thought Jasmine had gotten years younger when we saw her getting off the yellow submarine. Where's this secret fountain of youth, Jasmine?"

"Thanks, Joe. I'll have to disappoint you, though. There's no secret fountain there. I've been doing a bunch of different things while trying to keep healthy and sane. Thanks to a friend, I've been approaching my body and mind in some new ways."

"That sounds intriguing," I said, encouraging Jasmine to tell us more.

She continued, "I'm not making excuses for my infamous punctuality, but that's the reason I was a bit late coming here today. I was floating."

"Floating?" Gina queried.

"Yeah, floating. Like swimming. But, in a sensory deprivation tank."

"WHAT?" we all exclaimed.

"Is that the legal word for a large bathtub?" Neil laughed while taking a jab at Jasmine being a lawyer.

"No," she smiled back. "You should try it sometime. I first heard about it from my yoga instructor. Think about how many senses we all have. Five, right? Sight, smell, sound, taste, and touch. Now think about how many are active right now. At this exact moment."

"We're eyes wide open, so, sight's on," Neil volunteered, getting the ball rolling.

"And I can smell the food. Smell, check," I added.

"We can hear each other, and we're sipping our drinks and eating. That takes care of sound and taste. And we can feel our feet on the ground, and our fingers around our glasses, so that covers touch too, right," Jasmine said, looking at us.

We nodded, as she continued, "In short, we are engaging all our senses at this moment. Now, let's start subtracting. Can you imagine no taste?"

"That's easy," I volunteered. "When we're not eating."

"Exactly," Jasmine said. "Can you imagine no taste, smell, sight, or sound?"

We all thought for a moment.

"When we're sleeping," Neil volunteered.

"Not when you're sleeping, Neil," Gina chuckled. "Your snoring takes care of enough sound."

We all laughed as Neil feigned mock-hurt. He added, "OK, not my sleeping then. Meditating?"

"That's correct," said Jasmine. "Sleeping and meditating both work."

"So, we've knocked off four senses," Jasmine continued. "And that's great. It's always good to give our senses a break, especially given how over-stimulating our world is. Now, here's a real challenge. The fifth, touch, is the toughest to switch off. If you're sitting, you feel the chair. If you're standing, you feel the ground beneath your feet. If you're sleeping, you feel the bed under you. Can any of you imagine a situation when we don't feel anything at all?"

We all pondered as Jasmine looked at us with the expression of the host of a TV quiz show.

"In space?" Joe asked.

"I was about to say that. You beat me to it," Gina added.

"Great point," Jasmine encouraged. "How about on earth? It's going to be some years before we're all space-bound."

"The tank?" Neil exclaimed, connecting the dots. "You said something about a tank. And floating. In a tank of water?"

"Yup. Absolutely," nodded Jasmine. "Exactly what a sensory deprivation tank does. True to its name, it literally deprives your senses. Think of it as a large bathtub."

"So, I got that one right," Neil observed, complimenting himself.

"Yes, but one that can be closed," Jasmine continued. "So, sight, sound, smell, and taste are knocked off the menu. The water has a few hundreds of pounds of Epsom salts dissolved in it, making it dense."

"Like the Dead Sea?" I asked, increasingly fascinated by what Jasmine was describing.

"Yes, Kai. Exactly like the Dead Sea. With one little twist. The temperature of the water in the tank is maintained at standard body surface temperature. That way, when you're floating inside your little chamber, the physical boundaries between you and the water around you dissolve, and you become one with the world."

"OK, now that last part sounds like a lot of mumbo-jumbo," Neil said, skeptically.

"Don't knock it till you try it," Jasmine retorted. "I was skeptical too, at first, when my yoga instructor, Mary, told me about it. I'd previously heard it mentioned on a podcast and dismissed it as a new-age mumbo jumbo too. On a whim, I gave it a shot. I wouldn't have imagined me doing something like this, considering that I always thought I was claustrophobic. But this was something else. It literally opened my mind."

"Sounds like you were floating in more senses than one, pun totally intended," Joe observed with a deadpan expression. He was never one to let an opportunity for lousy humor pass.

"Totally," Jasmine agreed, chuckling. "Later, I learned that flotation generates something called theta waves in the brain. Theta waves are usually observed just before falling asleep or right after waking up. They're associated with lucid dream states, creativity, meditation, and daydreams. Seriously, you all. Give it a shot. There's so much about our bodies we are yet to discover."

"Wow. That's some journey inside, Jasmine," Neil said. "And, here I was thinking I was achieving theta states by traveling outside."

"Traveling? Outside?" Jasmine exclaimed.

"Didn't you get the lockdown memo? How were you traveling?" Joe added.

"Ask me about it," Gina chimed in. "I've been glad that Neil's been getting out and about. His hyperactivity would have chewed his brains, otherwise. And ours."

"That's true," Neil admitted. "So, I've now discovered a new-found love for the outdoors."

"You? Outdoors?" Jasmine asked incredulously. "I thought your definition of the outdoors stopped at malls with skylights?"

"I did, too," Neil admitted. "That's changed quite a bit, thanks to my friend, Trey. Do you remember him? We had him over once when you all were here too before this whole pandemic happened."

"The Bob Marley guy? Your SoundCloud buddy?" Joe asked. "He's pretty chill."

"The same guy," Neil confirmed. "Turns out that he's into a bunch of other things too—travel and the outdoors, for starters. We discussed some new loops I was working on when I admitted that my creativity had taken a hit perhaps due to being cooped up in the house. He encouraged me to get outside, and I had the same question you all asked me. Outside? How?"

"So, how?" I asked, curious about how Neil and Trey circumvented the travel constraints that had been in place.

"Camping. When Trey first mentioned it, I clarified that I couldn't pitch a tent to save my life. He explained that the world had changed to accommodate folks like me. He introduced me to glamping where you book tents as you'd book a hotel room. I tried it a couple of times. And then, a few more. Pretty soon, I was hooked. I've camped on hills, at sites near streams and lakes, and in the middle of pastures with never-ending green. It's been an eye-opener. I even graduated to buying camping gear, and now I've started camping out on my own."

"Wow," Joe exclaimed. "Gina, the boys and you go as well?"

"The boys do sometimes. Me, less often. Neil's done a bunch of solo trips too. And we were both glad for the space," she said sagely.

As we all knew, Neil and Gina had an enviable relationship, honed over twenty-five years of being together. While they had some common interests, they had many individual ones too and ensured that the other had the time and space for their respective personal journeys.

Neil added, "Nowadays, each time I'm stuck with a particularly thorny problem, an idea, or a piece of music or writing I'm working on, camp-time it is. Time to pick my trusty tent, sleeping bag, stove, and camp chair, and head to the nearest patch of non-urban green."

"Who'd have thought?" Jasmine said, amazed at Neil's transformation from urban city-slicker to a child of nature. "Neil, you and the outdoors. Now, this is a side of you I had no clue about."

"Me neither," Neil quipped.

"Speaking of the outdoors," I said, breaking my self-imposed silence. "Anyone else feeling a bit cold?"

"Yes, it's getting a bit chilly. Let's go inside," Gina said. "Take your drinks into the study. And dinner's ready when we are."

We took her cue and moved inside from the deck and paused at the kitchen to refill our drinks. After what seemed like ages, we were absorbing Gina and Neil's cozy home with its simple and minimalist aesthetic. None of us had been inside anyone's homes for a few months. We remembered how different parts of their home reflected their individual and collective personalities and their many journeys as a family with their now-adult sons.

Art and memories of different shapes and frame-sizes adorned the walls and nooks of their study in a seamless way. Ranging from cigar-cases from Cuba to statuettes from Cyprus, they all felt like they belonged there in a way that compressed different places and times into a 'here and now.' The study, a three-hundred square-foot space, was the venue of many eventful evenings in the past and was exactly as I'd last remembered it.

Or, so I thought.

"Hey, check that out. That's new, isn't it?" Jasmine exclaimed.

"Is it?" Joe asked, looking at the writing desk she was pointing at.

"Trust you to notice, Jasmine. And you, not to, Joe," Neil laughed. He continued, "Meet my new writing table, aka creative nook, remade, and refurbished by a local master craftsperson."

Neil's new table was what was, for reasons I never understood, called a secretary table. It was compact but functional and exuded an old-world charm. The walnut veneer and the fold-out table with its brass ring drawers would have fit right in at the set of a British period drama.

"It looks pretty cool. And I didn't even know there were local craftsmen anymore," Joe exclaimed. "I thought they were a dying breed."

"Craftsperson," Neil corrected.

"And hyper-local. In. This. Room," Neil added for effect as he looked appreciatively at Gina before stepping into the kitchen to refill the bowl of guacamole that we had finished in record time.

Three pairs of eyes followed his.

"You?" Jasmine asked, looking at Gina. Her tone of voice betrayed her disbelief.

Since college, she'd known Gina, and like Joe and me, had never thought of Gina as a woodworker. Creative person? Yes. Sanding-machine operator? No.

Gina blushed. Like Joe, she shunned the spotlight.

"Blame it on HGTV," she laughed, referring to the home-improvement channel that was all the rage, especially during the lockdown. Ironically, people were watching more shows about houses while constrained within their own.

Gina added, "After hours of watching upcycling shows on TV, I decided I'd try my hands at something. Some time ago, I'd bought this old, broken-down desk for a song at a local flea market. I always planned to refurbish it even if I hadn't the faintest idea how. I mean, I knew I wanted it to look like it does now—a contemporary look on furniture from a bygone era."

"That it has, for sure," I commented. "It reminds me of British serials from the nineteenth century."

"I'm glad," Gina smiled, accepting the compliment. "At first, I had no idea how to do it. Sanding, stripping, staining were all alien terms a few months ago. Several episodes of HGTV and a few YouTube videos later, I finally mustered the courage to work on it. Neil even gifted me an online woodworking course for my birthday. His alternating between goading and encouraging me might have helped too. But don't ever tell him that."

"Don't tell me what?" Neil asked as he returned with the guac and some tortilla chips.

"Nothing major," Jasmine said, winking at Gina. "Gina was telling us how this amazing masterpiece came to be and how you're going to write your next big book on this."

"On this and under a tent," Joe corrected, as we all laughed.

I managed a suppressed smile. I'd listened to my friends' new avatars and journeys with admiration and a tinge of regret that my face betrayed.

"What about you?" Neil asked me. It was a question I had hoped not to answer.

"Yeah, you've been unusually quiet this evening, Kai. All good?" Jasmine added.

"All good. I think," I said, hesitantly. "Look at all of you. All these new dimensions to your personalities are fascinating. It almost feels like I don't know you anymore. It seems like you're new people. New improved people. Your version 2.0.

"What about me, you asked. Well, I cleaned the house. A lot. In ways that would have made Marie Kondo proud," I said, referring to the Netflix show on tidying up that made 'spark joy' a part of society's vocabulary.

"And I was pretty proud of it. Until now. After hearing all the fantastic stuff you all described, I believe I should have been more productive with my time during the lockdown. I have nothing to show for it."

"Hey, this isn't a contest," Neil quipped.

"I certainly wish you'd clean more, Neil," Gina laughed, hoping to lighten my mood with humor.

Joe reassuringly put his arm on my shoulder, "Hey, I've known you for a few decades now. You've been the competitive type right from our school days but do go easy on yourself, OK. As Neil said, it's not a contest."

"I know," I said. "It's just that after hearing from you all, I must admit that I felt I should be doing more with my life. I feel it ever so often, but this evening brought it up to the surface.

"Oh, and speaking of our school days, Joe. Guess what I found when I was cleaning up," I added.

Having downed the collective mood like a damp squib, I was trying to change the topic. I gingerly pulled out a folded sheet of paper from my jeans. Its sepia tones and texture betrayed its age. The faint double red lines on top and blue lines below were reminiscent of ruled notebooks from a bygone era. From a time when there wasn't something called the internet.

"As I said, I was cleaning up when I found this. And boy, it sure brought back memories," I said as I handed it to Joe to take a closer look.

A huge smile lit his face as he realized what he was looking at.

He whispered to himself, *"Name, Place, Animal, Thing."*

"Yup," I said.

"Name, Place, Animal, Thing," Joe exclaimed again, this time with a child-like squeal. "I haven't seen one of these in ages. This brings back memories. You must have had this for…"

"More than thirty years," I said, completing his sentence. "Yeah, it's over three decades since we last played this game when we were kids."

"Name, Place, Animal, Thing. What's that?" Gina asked.

"Sounds intriguing. Tell us more," Neil added.

"Can we play it?" asked Jasmine.

They all seemed relieved to change the subject and see me cheer up a bit. And they were curious about what Joe and I were all excited about.

"Sure," I said, looking towards Joe for encouragement.

"If you haven't played NPAT, you haven't gotten an education," Joe teased.

"Allow us to introduce you to a beautiful game, Name, Place, Animal, Thing. We need to start way back at school," I said, with the flourish of a master of ceremonies announcing the opening act at a Broadway show.

* * *

"Do you realize that all great literature is all about what a bummer it is to be a human being? Isn't it such a relief to have somebody say that?"

— Kurt Vonnegut, Jr.

Chapter 3

A Game

Joe and I spent most of our childhood in Dubai, where we were both typical expat kids whose parents were working at the rapidly growing desert city in the early eighties. I remember the exact year—1983. The year I became a teenager, and also the year when Michael Jackson released *Thriller*. It was a year when imaginations soared to space as *The Return of the Jedi* ran to packed theaters worldwide.

Back on Earth, daytime temperatures in the Middle East would regularly hit 40 degrees centigrade. That's over 104 degrees Fahrenheit—not the best time to be a kid on a school bus that didn't have air-conditioning. To keep our minds off the heat, the desert air, and the impending school day, we would amuse ourselves by playing games during the drive. One of the most popular games was Name, Place, Animal, Thing. Looking back, we were pretty unimaginative with naming things in those days.

The game was simple. And beautiful.

Every player would have a sheet of paper and a pencil. Or a pen, if you were older. Everyone's sheet would have four columns, titled Name, Place, Animal, and Thing.

For each round of the game, we'd take turns for one person to be the alphabet reciter who would recite the alphabet as fast as they could "A B C D E F G HIJKLMN…"

The person to the left of the *reciter* would be the *stop-watcher*, who would have the reciter *start* puking out the alphabet. A little later, the stop-watcher would then say *stop* to have the reciter stop.

The letter the reciter stopped at would be the letter in play.

Let's say it was the letter, T. Every player would have a minute to write a name, place, animal, and thing beginning with the letter T.

When the minute was up, it was pencils down and time to compare answers and compute scores.

If you had written a word that no one else had written, you'd get ten points. If more than one person had, say, Tiger, under Animal, each of them would only get five points. And needless to say, if you couldn't think of top, tank, thong, tourniquet, or anything else for a thing beginning with T, you'd get 0 points.

Points would be added, scores would be compared, and a new alphabet reciter would spit out the alphabet for a new round.

ABCD...

NAME	PLACE	ANIMAL	THING	
Jake 10	Japan 5	Jackal 5	Jacket 10	30
Sia 10	Stockholm 10	Sea Lion 10	Sea Salt 10	40

Looking back at my sheet of paper, I realized I'd explained the game with the enthusiasm of a thirteen-year-old. My friends were listening with rapt attention and amusement.

Joe chimed in, allowing me to catch my breath.

"*Name, Place, Animal, Thing* sure brings back some amazing memories. Underlying NPAT, as some of us called it, were interesting life lessons," he said philosophically.

"Name would kick things off on a high note. Everybody usually got ten points on Name as any pronounceable sequence of letters, one could argue, is a possible name of a person."

Joe continued, "For example, let's say we're on J, and instead of Joe, I wrote the name *Jacintoramen*? I could argue that if a South American ramen loving couple had a son, that's what they'd name him. Embedded within the creative names we'd come up with was realizing it was a big world. No name was strange."

As we grew up and traveled and worked and met different people from different cultures, we realized that was true. No name was strange, even if you couldn't pronounce it right.

I added, "Place conjured up images of faraway lands. When someone had an exotic place written down that no one else had heard about, they were obligated to tell a bit about the place to prove it existed. I remember a game when we had the letter D. Two of us, smug in our knowledge of geography, wrote *Djibouti*, and got five points each. The kid who didn't bother to think beyond writing *Dubai*, where he lived, was the only one who got a full ten points because no one else had written that. Everyone else was too smart for their own good."

"Sometimes, it pays not to overthink things," I paraphrased.

Joe added, "*Animal* included the entire animal kingdom—reptiles, mammals, birds, aquatic creatures, bacteria, amoeba, dinosaurs, and more. Over arguments and debates on whether an answer was an animal, we'd meander through discussions on cells and organic matter. And DNA. And existentialism. Essentially, what it means to be an animal. Of course, all hell would break loose when we got the letter X."

I told the group that *Thing*, like *Name*, was low-hanging fruit. With creative double words like telephone-pole or tent-peg, you could almost assure yourself of ten points on this. This universe of obscure objects painted a canvas of a world teeming with things to see and things to do. It was also funny how once you had an initial thought on a thing, it was often difficult to think beyond it. And then, when you read all the fantastic things others had written, you'd wonder why none of them came to your mind, familiar as they were.

"Oh, and in case you're still thinking about that animal beginning with the letter X," I added, "there's Xenon, a slender-billed rain forest bird from the Americas. There's also Xerus, a type of ground squirrel from Africa."

"And," I continued. "This is a big *And*. We learned all this before Google."

"Heck. Even before the internet," Joe added with gusto.

Jasmine, Gina, and Neil were smiling indulgently.

"Look at you both," Gina said. "Back to being kids."

"They never grew up," Jasmine quipped.

"We should play it sometime," Neil said. "Or tell our kids about it."

"Hey, your kids are adults now," Joe reminded him. "And come to think of it, kids these days have games that paper and pen will find hard to compete with."

"Unfortunate but true," said Gina, noticing that I was lost in thought again.

She raised her brows in my direction by way of asking the others to look out for me. They caught me staring at the paper in my hand with a faraway look.

"A bitcoin for your thoughts, Kai," Gina said.

"I'll take that," I laughed. "Something serendipitous occurred to me. I see things."

"Yeah, what's that? When you say you see things, you sound like that kid in the movie, *The Sixth Sense*," Neil chuckled.

"It just hit me that we've been talking about *Name Place Animal Thing* all this time. All. This. Time. Ever since this evening began."

Joe had a confused expression as did the others. "You mean, we've been talking about it for the last ten minutes or so since you showed that sheet of paper?"

"No, Joe. All this time. Ever since we were outside when you first told us about your becoming an EMT," I said.

"OK, now we're all confused," Neil said, echoing the look on everyone's faces.

"Hear me out," I implored.

"Joe is now an EMT. That's a new title for him. A new role in society, aka, a new *Name* that we now know him by."

"OK, I can buy that," Gina agreed.

"Neil's traveled to *Places* with his camping adventures."

"That's true," Joe said, already computing where this was headed.

"Jasmine," I started.

"If you call me an animal, I'll slap you," Jasmine laughed.

"I wouldn't dare," I continued. "But, what you said about our senses and sensory deprivation, one could argue, translates to simply *being*. Like a living, breathing—wait for it—*Animal*."

"That's so true," Jasmine agreed. "When I was in that tank, the sound and feel of my heart thumping was the only thing I heard and felt."

"And Gina made a *Thing*?" Neil asked rhetorically.

"Your new writing desk. Exactly," I said. "The four of you, my dear friends, had fantastic experiences in the last few months. Experiences around names, places, animals, and things. And after you shared them, I pulled out a sheet of paper with those same four words on it. If this isn't magical, what is?"

Everyone felt it. At that exact moment, the air-conditioner fan, obeying its hourly schedule, stopped and lent a poignant silence to the moment.

My friends and I were struck by the uncanny connection between their disconnected experiences and a childhood game from over thirty years ago. And I was chuffed. I was proud of myself for discovering this connection.

"I must admit that I feel a little less upset about my lack of any major accomplishments," I said, loudly breaking the silence.

"And you know what," I continued before any of my friends could interrupt and reassure me. "This is a sign. I'm going to use *Name Place Animal Thing* as my compass. My compass to guide me to a fuller life. That's the expression I was searching for—a fuller life."

"S.L.A.P., Kai," said Jasmine.

"Slap? I thought I dodged that one, Jasmine? I didn't call you an animal."

"SLAP's short for Sounds Like a Plan," Jasmine laughed, as I took her bait.

"It sure does sound like a plan," Gina added. "Do you know what you might want to do for each of these, though?"

"I knew I was missing something," I admitted. "It almost feels like the time I bought a full set of containers of different shapes and sizes at IKEA with no idea of what I wanted to put in them. I have four containers now titled Name, Place, Animal, and Thing. Next, I need to figure out what to fill each of them with."

"You should speak with Cora," Joe offered.

"Cora?"

"Yeah, my client. Remember? She's the person who told me about the EMT program. I enjoy each of our conversations, especially the ones that have nothing to do with work. She's got a pretty interesting perspective on work, careers, and life in general. You'll enjoy speaking with her, and I am happy to connect you both."

"Yay, you've got a *Name* guru," Jasmine cheered.

"I can help with *Place*," Neil offered. "I can't think of anyone better than Trey, my music buddy who introduced me to the outdoors. He's got earthy wisdom, pun intended, and some refreshing views on travel and seeing places."

"Now, that's what I call progress," I exclaimed. "Thanks, guys. Two down, and two to go. Not bad at all. I'm going to take the path of least resistance here.

Jasmine, can you help me with *Animal*? And you with *Thing*, Gina?"

"Sure," Jasmine said. "Mary's your girl."

"The deprivation tank lady?" I asked.

Jasmine chuckled, "You make her sound like a serial killer in a Netflix series. But yeah, Mary first told me about floating. She's my yoga instructor and is one of the most centered persons I've met. You'll feel it too when you meet her. There's something about Mary."

"Who's talking movie references now," said Gina. "And yes, I can help introduce you to someone helpful too. This guy called Vin, short for Vincent."

"Ah, yes, Vin. I agree. He's the right person," Neil added.

Gina continued, "We first met him at a PTO when our kids were classmates in high school. The first time we went to their house, we were amazed by how handy he was. He'd even built most of his house by himself. So, when I wanted to figure out how to make this table, he's the first guy I called to get a primer on painting and woodwork."

"A primer on painting," I noted. "You're effortlessly making woodworking jokes now. This guy, Vin, must be inspiring. Can you introduce me, Gina?"

"Ha, ha. I sure can. And by the way, he's into a bunch of things besides carpentry. I'll introduce you ASAP as he mentioned he was planning a holiday in the Caribbean with his wife. They never got to celebrate their empty-nester status with the pandemic around the same time their kid graduated from high-school. So, you might want to try and catch him before he leaves."

"I'd love that."

"Well, congratulations," Joe said, raising his glass of seltzer and speaking on behalf of everyone. "Not bad at all. This might be the most productive evening of your life. You've got a plan and people to help you along. What more could you ask for?"

"Certainly, seems like it. With a little help from my friends," I agreed, raising my glass along with the others. "Where's Gina disappeared to?"

Neil pointed to the dining room where Gina was speaking to someone on her cellphone. She raised her glass from afar and gave me an encouraging smile.

"I think *Name* is the last thing I should think about," I said, after some thought. "Intuitively, it feels like a later part of the journey. I'd think that doing things, seeing places, etcetera, paves the way for figuring out

Name. What do you think, Joe? How did you decide on this EMT thing, for example?"

"You're correct about your approach," Joe nodded. "Besides the circumstances around the pandemic and my conversation with my doctor-cousin, there were other parts I skipped. To cut a long story short, I realized that I was always inclined towards the medical profession."

"I remember quite well," I added. "I recall the time we finished high school when you were torn between choosing to become an engineer or a doctor."

"Yeah, you're right," said Joe. "And later, I found myself wishing that the coin flip turned out differently. Recently, I started doing some online courses at Coursera on biology and related fields. I also took a first aid course with the Red Cross. That was fortunate besides being fun. It turned out that Basic Life Support is a prerequisite for becoming an EMT. So, yeah, a bunch of things needs to fall into place before deciding what you want to spend more time with and to make it a vocation like I have."

Joe was interrupted by Gina who had just finished her call. "Hey Kai, I just got off a call with Vin. He's leaving on his holiday in three days, but he's happy to speak with you briefly over a Zoom call tomorrow."

"Wow, that was fast," I said, thankfully. "Looks like I'm actually on my way, folks. I already feel different."

"Sounds like a plan," Neil offered, raising his glass to me.

"Absolutely," I agreed, raising my glass to Neil. And to Gina, Joe, and Jasmine who'd joined the impromptu toast.

"To old friends and new teachers. Here's to names, places, animals, and things!"

* * *

"Ignorance killed the cat; curiosity was framed!"

— C.J. Cherryh

CHAPTER 4

Thing

❧

Considering he could fit engineering, painting, architecture, aviation, sculpture, and a dozen other things into an Italian summer, Leonardo Da Vinci was the original polymath.

I always wondered what his workspace might have looked like. Vin's workshop gave me a semblance. In fact, the first time we met, I renamed him "Vinci Vin" in my head.

The first thing I noticed on our Zoom call on Sunday morning was that Vinci Vin had more wires around his head than the hair on it. He was seated on what appeared to be a barstool in what seemed to be his garage or rather, what was once his garage. Wires and cables of varying lengths, gauges, and colors hung everywhere they could. An array of tools that would have put a hardware store to shame was dotted across the room like sprinkles on a birthday cake. Wood pieces of varying types, shapes, and sizes were stacked in bundles that had some unobvious logic behind them. Transparent boxes neatly arranged on shelves seemed to contain every screw, nut, bolt, rivet, and fastener known to man. Well, to carpenters at least.

The second thing I noticed was his smile. It flowed from kind eyes—the eyes of a person who found joy in simple pleasures.

"So, you're Kai, Gina's friend?" he bellowed. "Delighted to meet you."

He sounds like a character from the Victorian age, I remember thinking to myself.

"Likewise. Yes, I'm Gina's friend. Thanks for making the time for me and that too on a Sunday."

"You're welcome. And I'm glad we're talking," Vin said. "Our world needs more makers."

"Oh, I'm not a maker by any stretch of the imagination," I interrupted.

"Not yet. But you want to be one and that counts. The world is skewed towards consumption. Consuming can be a never-ending pursuit, especially for stuff and for entertainment. You can thank Amazon and Netflix for that. The world needs more makers, and starting to think about becoming a maker is obviously the first step towards actually becoming a maker."

"Think about it," he continued, with almost evangelistic zeal, "society has stopped innovating. Sure, we're churning out apps in truckloads, but fundamental discoveries and inventions of the kind we've had in the last two centuries? No, sir. Those have slowed down to a trickle. The internet has a lot to do with it. The way I think about it, every new day, every individual gets 86,400 new seconds to spend."

"Unfortunately," he lamented, "Every new company is figuring how to monetize those seconds. We need makers. So, once again, young Padawan, I'm glad you want to make things. Where would you like to start?"

Young Padawan, I thought to myself. I'd celebrated my fiftieth birthday three months ago on Zoom. No one had, in recent times, called me a young anything. The Jedi reference was a bonus. I was thrilled that Vin, who at the most, would have been ten years older than me, was a Star Wars fan. The force was strong with this one.

"Uh, that's part of the problem, Vin. I don't know where to begin."

"Analysis paralysis, analysis paralysis," Vin said, shaking his head. "I see it all the time. We overanalyze things, and overthink pros and cons, and never get off those starting blocks. Don't. Please don't."

"Errr. OK. But how?"

"Close your eyes," he instructed.

"Right now?"

"Yes, please," he said.

I did. It felt strange to have my eyes closed on a Zoom call with someone I'd met ten minutes ago.

"Now, tell yourself that you promise not to overthink things at this moment. I'm sure a bunch of ideas about things to make and do have come and gone through your head. Think about the most recent ideas that you've had and pick one. Or, at most, two for now, and decide on one of them by tomorrow. Please don't open your eyes until you've done this."

Spending more time with my eyes closed while Vin watched me over his iPad felt strange. It forced me to make up my mind much faster than I otherwise would. I think Vin knew this would happen.

And, he was right. I had no shortage of things I wanted to make and do. I had a commitment problem—a problem with deciding which of these ideas was 'worthy' of my time.

I opened my eyes to find Vin smiling. I detected a hint of mischief in his expression. He was obviously enjoying my discomfort.

I started, "So, I'm thinking of two…"

"Let me stop you right there," Vin said. "I don't want to know what. But I do want to see it next weekend."

"I'm off on a brief holiday tomorrow to Puerto Rico," he added. "So, how about we catch up next Saturday, almost a week from today? We'll meet over coffee. I missed cafes during the pandemic. I'm making up for lost time," he guffawed.

"OK, I guess," I said unconvincingly.

"Splendid. Shall we say 4 p.m.?"

"Uh. Sure. My weekend is quite open."

"What you make, see I will," he said, channeling his inner Yoda.

"Thanks a bunch for this, Vin. And safe travels," I smiled before clicking the big red button on my screen to end our call.

In less than sixty seconds, I was in a state of panic.

"What was I thinking?"

"What's wrong with me?"

"Why did I listen to Gina?"

"Should I make an excuse and duck out of this?"

I hadn't lied to Vin. I did have two ideas on things to make. The lockdown would have been a great time to start on them, but work seemed to expand to fill all the commuting time I'd saved. They were the most recent things I'd thought of, and hence the first to pop into my mind. Now, I wasn't sure anymore. I should have closed my eyes longer, weird as it felt.

Analysis paralysis, Vin's sage voice echoed in my head.

He was right. I did have a commitment problem.

I'd break that habit right now.

I would decide between making French pastries and building something electronic on an Arduino board.

I'd always enjoyed preparing the occasional elaborate meal, but French pastries were a few rungs higher than anything I'd tried. In recent months, I'd rediscovered my love for cooking but, apart from the occasional detour, I stuck to tried and tested recipes. My recipes were scarce on precision—something I'd heard was a cornerstone of French cuisine. A friend, a chef, once told me how fastidious French cooking was, and that making something as trivial as an omelet was a skill acquired over several weeks.

Learning to make French pastries would be like jumping off the deep end to learn swimming. I pictured myself balancing a tray of pastries while walking into a Starbucks. I felt like a scout about to sell cookies to raise funds. I also wasn't sure how amenable Starbucks might be to someone carrying food into their establishment.

The pastries don't make sense on so many counts, I said to myself.

Additionally, French pastries needed a lot of equipment and ingredients that I didn't have.

By the process of elimination, the Arduino it was.

I'd followed the Arduino and hobbyist electronics movement with fascination even though I'd done scant little about it. During my labs at school, I'd immensely enjoyed the electronics lab, but I hadn't done any electronics work in decades.

Like the Raspberry Pi before it, the Arduino provided a path of least resistance for people to dabble in electronics and get started using a kit in a box. The kit came with everything needed to make small LCD screens that display text, alarm bells, dancing LED lights, etc. It was perfect. And, it had been on my mind for some time. Besides my curiosity, I wanted to be a role model for our daughter to be excited about STEM, the popular acronym for Science, Technology, Engineering, and Math.

A few searches on Amazon later, I found three kits.

Any of them would have been perfect.

But not for me.

Sunday evening

I had to read the reviews for each before making a decision. Many of the reviewers also shared pictures and videos of their projects. They were fascinating, and I went down various YouTube rabbit holes. I also found many other accessories that Amazon said were commonly bought together with the kits

I was considering. I researched some more. And, some more.

"Analysis paralysis," I said to myself before going to bed.

Monday

I finally placed my order during the lunch break.

Thank God for one-day-delivery.

Tuesday

Nothing delivered.

Amazon now said it would be delivered on Wednesday.

Wednesday, 6 p.m.

Nothing delivered yet. I called Amazon and was politely told there were some unavoidable delays since supply chains were just about roaring back to life. Electronics DIY kits were not considered essential goods.

I could get a refund or wait for another day.

I decided I'd wait although I was getting increasingly concerned about my ability to have something ready by Saturday and, in time, for my catchup with Vin.

Thursday, 7:43 p.m.

Finally, it arrived, said a notification on my phone. I opened the front door to find a package outside. Like a serial killer, I ripped the Amazon smiley on the box with a knife and took out the Arduino Uno R3 starter kit.

Momentarily, I was transported back to my college lab.

Thursday, 7:58 p.m.

Reluctantly, I kept the Arduino's components back inside their box and went back to the PowerPoint presentation I was working on. The next day was one of those back-to-back meeting days at work, and so I could get to play with my new toy only by Friday evening.

Friday evening

I drove back from work, giddy with excitement. I didn't even take off my tie as I opened the kit's contents and spread them out on the dining table.

It was stimulating.

30 minutes later…

It was confusing.

There was so much I needed to do before I could even start my first project. First, I needed to install the Arduino's IDE, short for Integrated Development Environment. Then, I needed to write code in the IDE and get the computer and Arduino to talk to each other.

Since when did electronics get so complicated? In my days, we'd just hook up a couple of wires and ensure we wouldn't get electrocuted.

It wasn't complicated, but it was overwhelming. Especially, since I was trying to do it in a hurry.

Especially, since it was Friday evening—family movie night.

I'd given my kids a lecture the previous week on the importance of honoring commitments. I didn't want to set a bad example by skipping the movie.

Disappointed with my lack of progress, I settled into the couch with my cauliflower crust pizza, and we rented *The Gentlemen*, a *Guy Ritchie* movie. At least the film was fun.

Saturday

I had reconciled to the idea of disappointing Vin with my lack of something to show. I was not used to reneging on my promises and felt terrible. At least, I tried. I was in the middle of a grocery run when I got a text from Vin.

Hey, looking forward to catching up. I'm in your neighborhood earlier in the afternoon. Would 2 p.m. work instead of 4 p.m.?

Sure thing. 2 p.m. works. See you then. Looking forward, I typed, not meaning what I said.

A few hours later, I walked into Starbucks, a brown paper bag in hand with the Arduino components inside. Vin was already there, monopolizing a table where he'd spread out various sections of the New York Times. The Saturday editions were substantial. And Vin seemed intent on reading every single word on it.

He looked up from his sea of newsprint as he noticed me come inside.

He looked even more Yoda-like in person. A tanned Yoda. He was in an old pair of jeans, loafers, and a well-worn *Electronic Frontier Foundation* sweatshirt that said:

Defend free speech.
Fight surveillance.
Support innovation.
eff.org

"Finally," I said, taking his outstretched hand. "I assume from the tan that you had a lovely holiday."

"Oh, I most certainly did. It was splendid," Vin laughed. "I got more sun in three days than I did in three months. Why don't you grab a drink and tell me about what's in that bag of yours? I'm curious."

"Sure, but brace yourself for some disappointment," I said, heading to the counter.

A few minutes later, latte in hand, I described my misadventure to Vin. I felt like I was giving a confession at church, and he had the expression of a teacher being told that the dog ate the homework.

He listened patiently before looking at the contents of my bag and saying, "R3. Wow. I didn't even know they'd advanced so much with the Arduinos. I'd dabbled with one of the early ones. I hadn't seen this one yet."

I wasn't surprised.

"So, what else did you think of," he continued. "I remember last week you'd started off saying you had two things in mind."

I explained my penchant for making French pastry and why I decided not to do that.

"Now, that, I would have been grateful for," he guffawed.

That easy laugh again.

"Relax. Breathe," he said kindly. "You're not at school. You won't be punished for not submitting your homework. And congratulations. You are now on the path to becoming a maker again. As kids, we were all makers. And then, somewhere along the way, we lost it. You are on the way to finding it again. So, that's great progress."

"Thanks to you," I said. "And yes, you're right. I remember this amazing book called *Things to Make and Do* that I'd read as a teenager. Whenever I was bored, I'd flip to a page, rummage around for the cardboard, glue, and stuff it needed, and make something new. And show it off to my parents and friends."

Vin added, "If you were to do that today, I guess you'd be posting it on Instagram."

We laughed together.

"Gina told me you once had a company called WebOrigami?" he asked, changing tracks.

"Yeah, some time ago, when I tried my hand at entrepreneurship for a bit. I can't believe she remembered," I said.

"Perhaps it was her way of telling me there's a maker inside you," he commented. "Why that name? Web, I get. Origami? That's the Japanese art of paper folding, isn't it?"

"That's right," I said.

"We were building a web application. So, I thought folding web pages into beautiful things was a nice metaphor."

"Indeed, it is," he simply said.

"And, I used to do Origami as a kid," I continued.

"Do you still remember it?" he asked. "I mean, could you make something now? Even better, could you teach me?"

I was about to say "No" but caught myself. It didn't feel right saying no, especially to Vin, who had been so generous with his time.

"Well, I can try," I said hesitantly. "It's been ages since I did any Origami, so I don't even know if I'll remember. I'll need some paper too."

"Oh, trust me, you will remember. It's all in there somewhere," he said as he tapped his head with one hand while rummaging through his pile of two pounds of the New York Times with the other.

He finally found what he was looking for. "There we are. I never read the Style section. As you can imagine from seeing me, I'm not much into style," he remarked. "Let's cut some squares out of this for your Origami. Best use of this section of the Times."

I played along.

"All right," I said as Vin and I each took a sheet of paper and removed a strip off the longer end to make them square. My sheet had Kim Kardashian on it. *Even better*, I thought to myself.

"How about we make a crane?" I asked.

"It's the symbol of Origami and the one you see gracing most Origami books and apps."

"A crane it is, then," Vin agreed.

We spent the next ten minutes in an almost meditative state. I was trying to recall sequences of folds and creases buried beneath mountains of meetings and conferences and the hillocks of everyday life.

Following my instructions and doing the same steps with his sheet of paper, Vin kept encouraging me and assured me I'd remember it.

Funnily enough, he was right. Though I made some wrong folds and creases, I could recognize that they were wrong and retrace my steps. It was like walking down an unfamiliar path knowing that a little further was all you needed to go to be certain it wasn't the right one.

2:42 p.m.

We admired our handiwork. A couple of people walking past our table also commented on our little craft project.

"Origami? Noice," one said. It was amazing how an object could be a catalyst for conversation and human connection.

"So, maker-san, how do you feel now?" Vin inquired.

I now felt like I was talking to Mr. Miyagi from *The Karate Kid*. Right after a *wax-on, wax-off* lesson.

"Great," I answered enthusiastically.

"I was astonished that I managed to remember everything even though I blundered my way through. And I'll admit, it felt nice to be folding paper again and to see that," I said, nodding my head towards the two cranes proudly perched on our table.

"Of course, I wish I'd completed my homework in time as promised. That's the competitive streak in me, I guess," I laughed.

Vin smiled, "You only needed a starter motor, my friend. And by the way, you did turn in your homework, as you call it, in time. Not that it matters, but you were to turn it in by 4 p.m. when we were originally scheduled to meet. It's not 4 p.m. yet, and there's your crane. So, congratulations. You did it."

"Dang," I smiled. "Thank heavens for technicalities."

Vin laughed, "Now's a good time to start thinking about creating your calendar of curiosities."

"A what calendar?"

"A calendar of curiosities. Simply put, a list of *things* you think you might want to make or do. Then, you decide which of them you want to try for size every three months. It's like the quarterly plans you probably do at work. Only, this is for *things*—for proactively and deliberately trying new *things*. And guess what, you already have two on your list—Arduino, and Origami. Maybe, that's all you want to explore this quarter. And then, three months later, explore new things. Or, go deeper into some old ones. Lather. Rinse. Repeat."

"That makes so much sense," I said. "But how do I choose and decide? Close my eyes like you made me do last week?"

"That works, too," he laughed. "Or you could use a thinking tool I created. It's called the Physical Fertilizer Model."

Vin was obviously enjoying talking in riddles.

"OK, Vin, out with it," I said. "You know you've tickled my curiosity with a name like that. Physical Fertilizer? Now we're into gardening, are we?"

"Gardening the mind, indeed," Vin said, while simultaneously getting up to grab some paper napkins.

"And yes, I do enjoy corny names. I'll explain in a bit. First, let's chat a bit about the shape of stories."

More riddles, I smiled to myself.

"It will all make sense, I promise," Vin said, almost reading my mind.

"Every story has a shape. A short story, a novel, a Hollywood blockbuster, an indie film, a TED talk, a presentation—they're all stories. Stories are our best way of building empathy. And stories have shapes. Some people call them narrative arcs. I prefer stories."

He added while sketching on a napkin, "Kurt Vonnegut has this delightful four-minute video you should see called the shape of stories. It was his master's thesis, which was rejected because it was too simple and frivolous. He says any story can be plotted. The vertical axis represents the good and bad stuff the characters experience over time. Time is represented on the horizontal axis. So, this here is Cinderella, for example."

Vin, like Vonnegut, had reduced this famous tale to a graph on a Starbucks napkin—simple, frivolous, and profound.

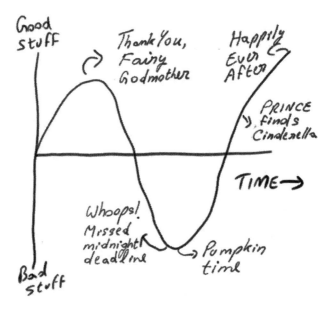

Vin continued, "Thousands of blockbusters have followed this exact shape. Some researchers found that most stories follow one of six shapes. Imagine that. All stories follow one of just six patterns."

"But, we digress," he exclaimed, "The purpose of this hopefully delightful detour was to show you the shape of your own story."

He started sketching on another napkin, "This is how you were over the last week. You went from having no prior knowledge on Arduinos to the joy of anticipation of a new adventure to the disappointment of perceived underachievement. And this is where you were about an hour ago."

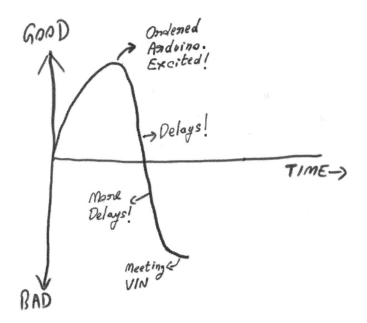

He continued while adding to his sketch, "And then, thanks to the Style section of *The Times*, this was the shape of your story over the last hour because you had some prior knowledge of Origami and acted on it."

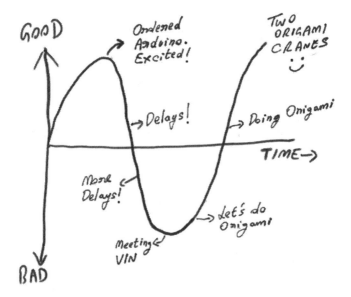

"Wow. Just wow," I said. I was fascinated by Vin's story about stories.

"And now for our *pièce de résistance*," he said with a mischievous glint in his eye. He put the two napkins next to each other and simply proclaimed, "Hello, Cinderella."

They were almost identical narrative arcs.

"Now that we've understood the shape of your stories," Vin said, "why do you think you were able to make progress with Origami but not with the Arduino?"

"I remembered some of my childhood Origami quite to my surprise. But, I didn't know anything about the Arduino, and a day was too short to learn?"

"Bingo," Vin said with the enthusiasm of a bingo organizer at a party. "You had some prior knowledge on one but no prior knowledge of the other."

"No Prior Knowledge—let's abbreviate it to NPK," he said as he opened another napkin and drew two axes on it. "At the other end of NPK is LPK, Lots a Prior Knowledge and SPK somewhere in the middle is…"

"Some Prior Knowledge?" I completed his sentence.

"You're catching on. And let's put the universe of things you can make on the other axis. They can be physical objects like these cranes. Or virtual stuff like an online game, or a podcast, or a blog post. All these need you to be a maker."

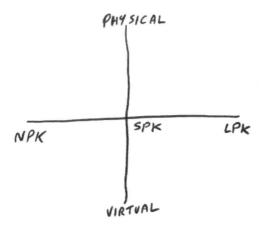

"That's an interesting way of looking at things to make and do," I agreed. "But, where's the fertilizer?"

"I was hoping you'd ask," Vin said with a wicked grin.

He continued, "If you remember your high school science, N, P and K are the chemical symbols for Nitrogen, Phosphorous, and Potassium. The three elements that sustain all plant life, also commonly known together as…"

"Fertilizer," I groaned with mock-exasperation.

"Vin, you take the cake when it comes to dad jokes. And I thought I was bad," I laughed.

"I have been accused of that. But voila. The physical fertilizer model," Vin said with a flourish.

"Now, I'd like you to place two dots on this graph. A dot to mark your crane and then a dot for the Arduino."

I thought a bit, smiled at myself and placed three dots…

"Very impressive," Vin agreed.

"Yes, the Arduino has a hardware part that's physical and a software part that's virtual. So, it deserves two parking spots, exactly as you've done.

"Now, please draw circles around the dots to represent the time and effort you think would go into each thing."

After a pause, I drew three circles as I said, "On second thought, I'd make my crane's circle even smaller."

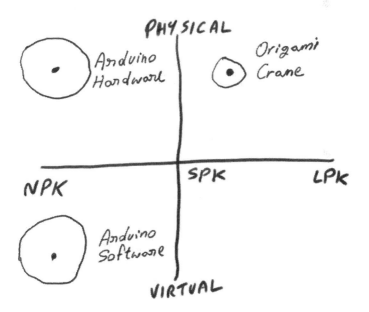

Vin nodded, agreeing, as he saw my handiwork. "Now, do you see why we could quickly achieve something by making the crane? Of course, you should do the Arduino too. Just remember that it will take more time.

As you learn more about the Arduino, it will move to the right where if you keep at it, in a few weeks, you'll have some prior knowledge.

"And in some months," he continued, "lots of prior knowledge. Needless to say, you'll have to invest the time in learning things about which you have no prior knowledge. That investment period can be frustrating as you will initially have little to show for your efforts. But afterward is when the magic begins."

I was nodding my head and grateful for all this wisdom.

Vin continued, "So, young Padawan, make a list of things you've wanted to do, things you've done in the past, things about which you've been curious. Anything. Everything.

"Then map them out as circles on a graph and pick one or two to do over the next three months. I wouldn't recommend more than three. Try and mix things up. Don't do many things that you need to learn from scratch. And do physical things too, like we just did. Getting your hands dirty is an underappreciated thing."

I was nodding vigorously and added, "I think I get it."

"That's what Gina did, right?" I said. "Sure, she had to learn about Tung oil and patinas, and she certainly had to get her hands dirty. But that beautiful desk she made for Neil is a testament to her becoming a maker."

"Exactly," smiled Vin. He added, "She moved from NPK, or having no prior knowledge on woodworking to some prior knowledge. So, anything new that she now does will take less time."

We spent the next thirty minutes chatting. We discussed a wide array of topics, including all the things I'd flirted with the thought of trying, the new world of online education, and the lost art of wondering. Vin shared his journey as a maker and how he was still learning something new almost every single day. He even shared some of his resolutions, including a recent one on eating healthy and exercising more. Vin promised to text me links to other online resources I would enjoy. In turn, I promised to find and send him some on Origami, which he said he'd enjoyed doing with me.

"Whoa, look at the time," Vin suddenly said.

"I've got to make my weekly pilgrimage to the hardware store. My weekend feels incomplete if I don't," he laughed.

"I'm not surprised. I'll hang around here for a bit," I said. I'd just gotten a fresh cup of coffee.

"Vin. Thank you. Truly," I said, getting up. "This has been an amazing afternoon. I've learned so much today."

He acknowledged my gratitude, "I wish you luck in whatever you choose to make. Give me a shout if you ever need any help. And remember, the world needs more makers. Spread the gospel."

I hugged Vin goodbye, overcome by gratitude.

After he left, I picked up the napkins he'd written on, and gingerly, like the pieces of wisdom that they were, placed them between the pages of my Moleskine notebook. *Cinderella*, I smiled to myself.

I sipped on my coffee as I looked at the two-dimensional sheets from *The New York Times*, now transformed into two beautiful three-dimensional cranes.

It had been an enlightening afternoon, and my mind was abuzz with all the things I'd always wanted to do, or had done some time in the distant past. I started writing them down in my notebook in no particular order, knowing they would gain perspective and priority when I placed them later in my physical fertilizer model. And from there, I would weave them into a quarterly calendar of curiosities.

I smiled in my mind at Vin's corny choice of name as I wrote: *Podcasting, Gardening, Magic tricks, Arduino, Molecular gastronomy, Stop-motion animation.*

"Mommy, mommy, look."

My thought-stream of things to make and do was interrupted by an excited little girl. She must have been about six years old. She was accompanied by a boy who, I assumed, was her younger brother. They had just walked into the cafe holding their mother's hands. Once safely inside, they were allowed to roam free and unhindered. Their young and curious eyes immediately zeroed in on our papercraft.

The girl and her brother saw the cranes and were about to reach for them with their outstretched hands when their mother said with a stern voice, "No. It's not yours."

I politely interrupted her, "It's fine. Don't worry about it. If it's OK with you, they can have them."

"Are you sure? You don't have to."

"Oh, I'm pretty sure. I plan to make more, anyway."

"Thanks," she said. "That's very kind of you."

"You're welcome," I said while reaching for the cranes.

"Trying to figure how you made it will help keep them occupied on the ride back home," she laughed. "I'm sure they'll try and open it out and fold it back again."

"I'd be glad if they did that. The world needs more makers," I smiled, handing over the cranes to the delighted children.

* * *

"Outside of a dog, a book is man's best friend. Inside of a dog it's too dark to read."

– Groucho Marx

CHAPTER 5

Animal

I was anxiously waiting for Jasmine's call. A part of my anxiety stemmed from not being comfortable with having a 'meeting' without a clear plan. The rest of it came from *Yogaphobia*.

The moment Jasmine's cheerful voice and face filled my screen over Facetime, I felt better and simultaneously worse. I felt better because that's how Jasmine, who had arranged this 'meeting,' generally made everyone feel. She had the gift of infectious positivity. I felt worse because I regretted my decision not to go with Jasmine in person.

Jasmine's description of sensory deprivation, of the time she floated in tanks filled with Epsom salts, made me reflect that sensory deprivation was my default state. It was not a positive thought. I knew that there was a connection with my physical self that had, so far, eluded me. Jasmine thought her Yoga instructor, Mary, could help.

Mary had very kindly said she could find a few minutes to chat after the Sunday morning '*Yoga in the woods*' class where Jasmine was a student. The class was at a wooded park, in an almost-perfect rectangle framed by rows of cedar trees and under the canopy of the shade that their shadows provided.

Years ago, I had dismissed Yoga as something I would never try for reasons I never bothered to reflect on. I worried that if I met Mary at '*her turf*,' Jasmine and she would somehow brainwash me into taking up Yoga. In retrospect, it was a needless worry.

Mary's class moved outdoors when the lockdowns happened and continued there even after things normalized. Everyone got so hooked to *Yoga in the woods* that they tried to have a couple of classes outside every week, weather permitting. When I saw the green background over my call with Jasmine, a part of me wished I were there and that I hadn't been so pig-headed about doing this over a call.

Jasmine had finished her session and seemed positively radiant. We were waiting for Mary, who was still addressing a couple of students' questions. Behind Jasmine, I caught glimpses of various students walking with rolled-up mats. They all seemed happy.

Finally, almost ten minutes after our scheduled time, I saw someone approaching the camera frame from behind Jasmine's left shoulder. She had a feline grace in the way she walked. From ten feet behind Jasmine, she started waving and smiling at the phone as though she was meeting an old friend.

"Hey, Kai. Nice to meet you. Even if not in person."

"You too. From the looks on Jasmine's face and some other students I saw on this call, your class is popular," I said.

"I can't complain. I've been very fortunate," she said as Jasmine handed over her phone to Mary and told me that she'd catch up with me later.

"Good luck," Jasmine said. "To both of you," she added with a smile.

Mary, now holding Jasmine's phone, said, "Isn't Jasmine awesome?"

"She is," I said, "but you must promise never to tell her I said so."

Mary laughed. She had an easy laugh not one of those manicured ones that were intent on sounding socially correct. Hers was wanton—the laughter of a child before the onset of adulthood and its perceived protocols.

"So, what are you searching for?" Mary asked, bringing my thoughts back to the reason for our conversation. She was looking at me with her deep blue-grey eyes. It seemed like she wanted to listen to what my eyes were saying rather than hear the words that I said.

"I'm not sure," I admitted. "I know that in the course of juggling many things, I've let some things slip on the health front. When I recently met up with some friends, we were all impressed with how centered Jasmine had become. She said you had a big role to play in it and suggested I speak with you. That's it."

I was looking at Mary in earnest, almost hoping my fuzzy but honest narrative made some sense.

She smiled and said, "I think I get it. The operative word here is *juggling*. Have you heard the analogy of how we're all juggling three balls at all times?"

"I haven't."

"It's quite simple," Mary continued. "At any point in time, we are juggling three balls. The first is that of health—physical and mental well-being. The second is that of relationships. This includes relationships with family, near and far, and relationships with friends.

"And finally, the third ball is that of finances. This includes your job, career, investments, the stock market, and everything. Of course, many may argue that their careers are their passion. Good for them, but finally, it is about a means toward financial security. Or to put it simply, finances."

I had my hand on my chin, and I was listening with rapt attention.

Mary continued, "Life is all about keeping these three balls up in the air. All. The. Time."

"Of course," she added, "being human, we'll drop some balls from time to time. Now, here's the catch. The finance ball that most of us focus on the most is made of steel. Drop it, and there will be a dent for sure. Pick it up again and juggle away.

"The relationships' ball is made of porcelain. Drop it, and it will break. There's nothing that a bit of super glue can't fix, but the cracks will show."

Mary completed her fascinating story, "The ball of health, my friend, is made of glass. Drop it, and unless you're fortunate, you'll have one less ball to juggle. So, yeah, getting some of that spotlight back on your health is a good thing to do."

"Wow," I said. "That sure puts things in perspective."

"It is a beautiful analogy," Mary acknowledged. "Someone I respect and who is a mentor of sorts first told it to me years ago. And yes, it does put life in perspective."

"Speaking of mentors, I owe you an apology," Mary said, looking at her watch.

"What for?" I asked.

"I know Jasmine scheduled this time for us to chat, but I'm afraid I'll need to leave soon as I'm running late for an appointment. I'm part of a volunteer group that teaches kids Yoga at an after-school center. The volunteer scheduled for today had to cancel at the last minute, and so I'm filling in. How about we continue our chat next week? You could come to my class here."

"Sure thing. Only, I'm not sure about class next week," I said, distractedly, as my dog entered the frame of my camera. My dog wondered why I had absconded from my duties of petting her every time we were on the couch.

I continued, "I'm free next Sunday, but to be honest, I don't think I'm into Yoga."

"No, silly," she said like we were old friends.

"I'm the last person who'll force someone to come to a class. I was suggesting we meet after my class—at the same time next week. And by the way, that's a lovely dog. What's his name?"

"Her name," I corrected, "is Nim. That's short for Nymeria."

"Isn't that the name of a dire-wolf in *Game of Thrones*?" Mary asked.

"So, I'm told," I admitted. "I'm not really into GoT, but my daughter is, and she chose the name."

"That's fantastic," Mary interrupted, obviously in a hurry. "Because it will be easy for you to do your homework before we meet next week."

"Homework?"

"Of course. Nothing comes easy," Mary said with mock sternness.

"Don't worry, though. It's pretty simple. It's less than twenty-seven words long."

"OK," I said suspiciously.

"Do you have any other pets?" she asked. I shook my head to indicate that I didn't.

Mary continued, "Fine. I want you to observe Nim. And when we meet next week, I want you to tell me three things she does that you don't. Three things that you do that she doesn't. And finally, three things that you both do."

"So, nine things in all," she summarized. "Each of them can't be over three words long. So, your homework, my friend, is only three times three times three—that's twenty-seven words at most over a whole week. How bad is that?"

"I'll admit it sounds reasonable," I said. "I feel there's a catch somewhere."

"We'll find out next week, won't we?" she smiled, before adding, "next week, same time, same place here, and don't worry, I won't ask you to hold a full pigeon-pose."

We were both smiling as she disconnected the call.

This homework thing was becoming a recurring theme with my friends' friends, I thought to myself. First Vin, and now Mary. I wondered if my friends were playing a prank on me through Mary, but the sage advice I'd gotten from Vin made me believe there were lessons to be learned here too.

Mary's homework was more challenging than I thought. It certainly made for an atypical week— for Nim, at least. I pulled out my trusty Moleskine notebook and turned the page over from my growing but stimulating list of things to make and do. I was already having a 'problem of plenty' for my calendar of curiosities, and I was glad for it.

What a difference a couple of weeks can make, I thought to myself.

I titled the new page "My dog." It was a throwback to my elementary school days when this was probably the title of an essay I'd written at that time.

Armed with my notebook, I set out to 'observe' Nim. I was on the couch, and she was sitting five feet away on the carpet with her chin on the floor, eyes ever alert. She was an anxious dog, and I imagine my impersonation of a psychoanalyst interviewing a patient didn't help. She regarded me with suspicion as I stared at her, trying to derive meaning from the mundane act of observing my dog.

I moved my hand to jot down a thought and that was enough to trigger something in Nim. She stood up in a flash, and scampered away, convinced that I'd lost it. I wrote my first set of nine three-word answers under the *Things Nim does that I don't* column.

Things Nim does that I don't	Things I do that Nim does not	Things that we both do
Moves really Fast		

The next day after work was similar. After I walked in, Nim ran up to me as she always did. After settling in, I was about to turn the TV on and sink into the couch when I remembered my homework. Nim was waiting to play with me, but instead, I stared at her. She stared right back. Our version of a Mexican standoff continued for a while. Finally, she simply walked away. She sensed something was off with me, but couldn't be bothered to find out.

The rest of the week saw some version of this interaction play out, and finally, at the end of the week, I had two columns filled out. These were the most challenging eighteen words I had written. The third and last column was relatively more straightforward, and I could wrap it pretty fast.

My homework was complete, and I was ready for the next day—curious about what *Manimal Mary* had to say.

In my head, and as I had done with Vinci Vin, given my penchant for alliterations, I had named her Manimal Mary. *Manimal* was the name of a corny TV show in the eighties, which, when I'd first seen it as a kid, felt like a well-made show. Its main character, Dr. Chase, was a shape-shifting man who could turn himself into any animal he chose and used this ability to help solve crimes. I later learned that *Manimal* had the dubious distinction of having made it to a famous list—the worst science fiction shows of all time.

My completed homework was a sheet of paper that I tore from the notebook.

Things Nim does that I don't	Things I do that Nim does not	Things that we both do
Moves really Fast	Exercise every day	MOVE
Absorbs her environment	Watch some TV	RELAX
Sleeps much more	Set an Alarm	SNORE

The first column did seem like one of my childhood essays on my dog.

I have a dog. Her name is Nim. She moves really fast. She absorbs the environment she is in. She sleeps a lot. I love my dog.

It felt childish.

On Sunday, I waited by the side of a cedar tree as Mary wrapped her class. Students were rolling up their yoga mats and chatting with each other. A couple of them seemed to be clarifying doubts about their postures with Mary. The weather was great, and I counted at least thirty students—more than I'd seen on our video call the previous week. Jasmine was traveling on work and hence skipped this class. Mary saw me waiting and waved to acknowledge me and convey that she'd soon join me.

Why a dog? I wondered to myself as Mary finished speaking with the last of her eager students and walked towards me.

She hugged me hello. "Good to see you again, and in person. Walk and talk?"

"Sure, and it's lovely to meet you too. Thanks for making time for me," I said as we walked alongside a row of cedar trees.

"So, about this homework that you gave me. I've been super curious. Why a dog?"

"Because you don't have a cat," she immediately remarked, unable to suppress a smile.

"OK, I give up," I said with mock-exasperation. "What does that even mean?"

"It's biology," she remarked. "Do you know that as a species, we aren't too different from many animals? We share ninety-nine percent of our DNA with chimps. It's a minuscule one percent that separates us from them. We share over ninety percent of our DNA with rats, and that's why they're used often for drug and vaccine testing. And it's eighty-four percent with dogs."

"What about cats?" I asked, suspecting she wanted me to ask precisely this question.

"Ninety percent," she answered with a fist bump into the air. "And that, if anything, should put an end to that eternal dog versus cat debate. Cats are genetically closer to humans than dogs."

"Let me guess," I smiled. "You have a cat."

"Guilty as charged," she said, before switching tracks back to my homework. "So, what did you learn from your dog?"

"First, that she doesn't like me staring at her. I thought she'd enjoy the attention, but she was more weirded out than I was."

"I'm not surprised. Animals can sense when something is different. Did you manage your twenty-seven-word homework?"

"Twenty-one. I didn't need all twenty-seven," I said while reaching for my pocket to fish out the sheet of paper on which I'd written my homework.

We broke our stride as she went through what I'd written. After half a minute that felt a lot longer, Mary smiled and finally spoke.

"What do you think about the things you wrote in your first column?" Mary asked.

"Almost envious," I said, finding it unexplainable that I'd envy my dog. I clarified, "I mean, I'd love to move faster, and I'd love to sleep more, for starters."

"So would I," Mary agreed. "And, absorb my environment in the way animals do so effortlessly. They seem to be able to be in the moment."

"That's so true," I nodded. "It also amazes me how often Nim stays idle—doing nothing."

"Great point," Mary said. "Doing nothing is a great thing. Animals can stay still and don't crave constant sensory stimulation as we do. Give a person a spare minute and they'll reach for their phone."

"Moving on to your second column," she continued. "If you're anything like me, I'm assuming you'll agree that these aren't amazing things about being human? We exercise almost because we have to, TV can be mind-numbing, and no one enjoys setting the alarm. We'd all prefer to sleep till our body wants to wake up, right?"

"I'd agree, even if my boss wouldn't," I said.

"This brings us to your last column," Mary said, "which, by the way, is amazing."

I confessed that the last column was the one I spent the least time on. I was almost frivolous with my answers.

"I thought they were three beautiful one-word answers," Mary smiled. "Coincidentally, your answers dovetail with what I like to call the BBB approach. Any guesses on what BBB might stand for?"

"The stores? Bed, Bath, and Beyond?"

"No," she laughed. "But good guess."

"Better Business Bureau?"

"Certainly not," she chuckled. "I'm going to stop you from offloading all your BBB expansions. BBB is short for the Body, the Brain, and what many believe is the connection between the two—the Breath. The secret to good health is ensuring you're always doing something to nurture each of the three."

"You make it all sound pretty simple."

"It is. Look at your answers again in your last column. Move, you said. Move what? Your body, of course. Relax, you've written. What needs to be relaxed? More often than not, your mind. And your funniest answer was that you and Nim snore. It's all about breathing. That's the reason why I loved your responses there."

"So, what does one do for the body, brain, and breath? Is there a way I should be approaching it?" I asked.

"I'm glad you ask. There is, indeed. It's a two-word answer. Any guesses?"

"Forty-two?" I answered, with an impish smile.

"You're funny. And I'm glad to know you're also a fan of *The Hitchhiker's Guide to the Galaxy*.

"But," I said, "I assume forty-two is not the right answer. So, what is?"

Mary stopped and turned towards me.

"*Go slow*," she simply said.

"That's it? What does that mean? Go slow?"

"Let me illustrate it with an example," she said. "Have you heard of 'the Linda problem'?"

"No, I haven't."

"Let's say I have a friend called Linda, a young, single, outspoken, and very bright lady, who, as a student, was deeply concerned with discrimination and social justice."

"OK," I replied, curious about where this was leading.

Mary continued, "What do you think is more probable—that Linda is a bank teller, or that she is a bank teller and an active feminist?"

"A feminist bank teller," I replied instantly. "I'm going with my gut here."

Mary smiled, "That is the Linda problem. Like you, most people say Linda's a feminist bank teller. However, that violates the rules of probability. It is more probable that Linda is a bank teller than a feminist bank teller because every feminist bank teller is obviously also a bank teller."

She paused to let it sink in.

"Oh, wow. Now I get it," I said after pondering for a bit over what Mary had explained. It was one of those things that were obvious in retrospect. "So, what does this have to do with going slow?"

"There's a lovely book called *Thinking Fast and Slow*. It's by Daniel Kahneman, a Nobel Prize winner in economics," Mary said.

"Since you weren't familiar with 'the Linda problem,' I assume you haven't read it?"

I admitted I hadn't and noted down the name of the book on my phone.

"Without getting into too much detail, his book says there are two modes in which we think. Kahneman calls them *System 1* and *System 2*. System 1 is fast, automatic, and almost unconscious. It's what you'd use driving a car on an empty road or when solving for, say, one plus one. System 2, on the other hand, is slow, effortful, and conscious. It's what you'd use when parallel parking into a tight space or solving for thirteen times twenty-eight."

She continued, "System 1 is also the part of your brain that enjoys that lazy scroll through a Facebook feed. It's your BuzzFeed brain that enjoys clickbait titles like 'Six reasons you'll never guess about why you are not losing weight'."

"You're a mind reader," I smiled. "I might have read that very article this morning at breakfast."

"System 1," Mary continued with a smile, "is relatively lazy and likes to substitute tough questions with easy ones. When I asked you about Linda, System 1 simply substituted an easier question—Is Linda a feminist? And that's why, like most people, you answered that she was more likely to be a feminist bank teller than a bank teller."

I understood, and added, "So, when you explained it, and I got it, that was System 2 working deliberately and thoughtfully, right?"

"Exactly! You were thinking slow then."

"Wow, this is interesting. I'm certainly going to read that book. What's going slow got to do with the breath?"

"Let's save the *breath* for last, shall we?" Mary asked, making an unintentional pun in the process. "Let's talk about the body first."

She continued, "The world has unfortunately gotten into thinking about the body from the lens of the fitness industry. Everything is either for cardiological fitness or strength training. Sometimes, some flexibility and stretching as an afterthought. Or a combination of new-fangled things, some new version of High-Intensity Interval Training."

It was evident that Mary had little regard for most of the fitness industry.

"Very few people talk about movement. Pure movement. Slow, deliberate, purposeful movement," she lamented. "I'm not plugging my class here, but that's what attracted me to Yoga. It helped me go slow with my brain, body, and breath. Of course, Yoga variants have borrowed from cardio, strength training, and HIIT, and sometimes combined these to give a different experience. But, the traditional approach that I teach is slow and deliberate."

"I think I get it," I said. "And yes, most fitness franchises out there are focused on getting your pulse racing in new and creative ways."

Mary interrupted me, "And that's not a bad thing by the way. We do need to get our pulse racing and do all those things. I'm only saying that we need to remember to *go slow* and deliberate at times."

"Which is a good segue into breathing," Mary added.

"The last part of the trilogy?" I asked.

"Indeed, it is. So, where do you breathe from?"

"My nose, of course. And my mouth too, I guess."

"That's not what I meant," she chuckled. "What part of your torso moves when you breathe?"

"I was about to answer with my stomach," I admitted. "But that would have been a *System 1* answer."

"You're a fast learner."

I deliberated before answering, "You know what, I don't know. I thought it was my abdomen, but I was observing now, and it could be my chest too."

"Don't worry too much about it," she reassured me. "Most people don't know, and most people, to be fair, breathe from many parts of their torso, but there are dominant patterns we're often unaware of. Some people breathe deeper and from the lower part of their abdomen. Some breathe into their chest. Marathoners breathe differently from sprinters. All I'm suggesting is that you be more aware of it, and remember to, once in a while, breathe slow."

"So, how does one breathe slow?"

"There are many ways," she said.

"You'll have to find what works for you. For some, it's practicing Yoga. Or meditating on their own or using an app to focus on the breath to calm the body and brain. That's what most meditation is anyway—going from breath to breath. You could do it on the couch, or as Jasmine tried recently, in a sensory deprivation tank where your body, brain, and breath all go slow."

"It all fits and makes so much more sense now. And speaking of deprivation, you deprived me of a reason to pull Jasmine's leg on her mumbo-jumbo," I complained.

"Again," Mary smiled as she continued, "I'm not saying fast-breathing is bad. It has a role. For example, take hyperventilation. That's fast-breathing where you're expelling carbon dioxide faster than you're inhaling oxygen."

"Of course," she added, "oxygen is good, but too much of a good thing can be bad. It's bad if you're hyperventilating from a panic attack. It's good if you're doing controlled hyperventilation for a martial art or skin diving, both of which use hyperventilation in interesting ways. It's good if you're breathing fast amidst a long tennis rally especially if you win the point after that."

"This is fascinating stuff," I said. "I never knew that the same breathing patterns applied to panic attacks, karate, tennis, and diving."

"Yup, the body is a fascinating place," Mary said, smiling. "We should visit it more often.

"When I suggested you go slow with the body, brain, and the breath, I was not suggesting that you always go slow. It is important to go fast too."

I interjected, "So slow and steady doesn't always win the race?"

"Not necessarily," she said. "I'd simply phrase it as 'Go slow, mostly.' And when you can go slow in your brain, body, and breath, simultaneously, that's when some serious magic can happen."

"Magic?"

"Yes. Magical experiences where the mind makes connections and jumps that it wouldn't make in conscious thought. The history of innovation is full of examples.

"Take Newton's figuring out gravity when sitting idle under an apple tree and resting. Then there's Archimedes who figured the principles of buoyancy when in a bathtub. And the lesser-known story of how Kekule figured the closed-loop structure of Benzene in a dream where he saw a snake grab its tail to form a closed loop."

"Wow, I didn't know that one," I exclaimed.

Mary had a sly smile, "Can you guess a phrase that captures what Kekule, Archimedes, and Newton did to go slow? You know the answer. You said it sometime back."

"What?" I looked at Mary, confused.

"I said this? Wait, wait. Give me a minute."

After about ten seconds, I exclaimed, "*Bed, Bath, and Beyond.* That's it. Kekule went to bed and dreamed up the answer. Archimedes in his bath, and of course, Newton went outside under the apple tree, aka, beyond."

"Very impressive," Mary said, softly clapping her hands. "And yes, nothing of significance was created or discovered by someone glued to their phone. I find it useful to think of everything we have discussed today as a six-pack towards remembering our inner animal."

"Six-pack? Like abs?"

"Interestingly, yes. You could think of it as abs—the upper one representing the body. The lower one is the brain—symbolic of how your gut is sometimes considered a second brain. And finally, the middle row for your breath. On the left side are the fast parts that we usually do."

She elaborated, "*Fast* movements to pack as much exercise as we can into forty-five minutes, *fast* breathing from constant fight or flight responses, and *fast* thinking that all the digital feeds, and the companies that promote them make money off."

"And on the other side," she said, softening her voice, "there's the canvas for the magic to manifest. *Go slow, mostly.* Think *slow*, breathe *slow*, and move *slow*."

I cemented Manimal Mary's BBB analogy into a six-pack visual in my head.

	FAST	SLOW
BODY	Speedy Movement	Conscious Movement
BREATH	Puffing & Panting	Mindful & Calm
BRAIN	Reactive = Thinking Fast	Deliberate = Thinking Slow

We walked some more as we spoke about health, meditation, and many other things, including the best wineries within an hour's drive.

Mary seemed to be an authority on that subject too. She had an eclectic mix of interests, was also a fan of escape rooms, and recommended some. In turn, I suggested some local comedy clubs to her that she hadn't been to despite her love for stand-up comedy. All in all, it was an enriching and educational Sunday afternoon.

Half an hour later, we were back at the parking lot adjacent to where Mary conducted her class.

"Look at the time!" she exclaimed. "I'm supposed to catch up with one of my students over lunch, this guy who's helping build a mobile app for my classes."

"I thought you didn't like mobile phones?" I teased.

"I never said that," Mary smiled, refusing to take the bait.

"All the best with figuring your journey," she said as we hugged. "Give me a shout if I can help."

"You know where to find me," she added, waving her hands in the direction of the cedar trees.

"I certainly will. Thank you so much, Mary. Today's been a mind opener of sorts. There's still one thing though—something I'm still not able to figure."

"What's that?"

"I can't think of one natural, human thing I do that my dog doesn't. It's been at the back of my head, and I can't believe I can't think of a single thing without it being something manufactured like watching TV or setting my alarm."

"What about laughing?" Mary asked.

"We spoke about comedy a little while ago. Have you ever seen your dog laugh?" she added. "Humans do it all the time. It's core to our lives—the occasional jokes, laughs, or chuckles."

"Yeah, that's correct," I said, after reflecting on what she'd said. "Animals don't laugh."

"Or so we think. Perhaps they do, in their way," Mary smiled as she waved me goodbye and wished me luck again.

The sun was overhead. It was a lovely day to be outside, and I remembered that I had a picnic mat in the car. I spread it out on the grass and lay down on it, looking up at the sky and allowing the sun to wash my face gently. It felt good. When it began to get a bit too warm for my taste, I turned around, lay on my stomach, and rested on my elbows with my back arched as I drank the sounds and sights around me. I smiled as I recalled Mary doing something similar with her students towards the end of class. She called it a *Cobra pose*. I could smell the ground and fresh grass. I even saw a dragonfly hover above some blades of grass, like nature's own helicopter. In the distance, I spotted a group of people poetically moving their bodies in what I assumed were Tai Chi movements. Except for two teenagers, most of them seemed to be in their sixties or older. The group was beautiful to watch. It was like a gentle choreographed dance.

They were going slow, as was I, that beautiful afternoon.

* * *

"Traveling is the antidote to ignorance."

— *Trevor Noah*

CHAPTER 6

Place

On Wednesday evening, upon hearing the furious splashing of water and his voice in staccato bursts, I worried that Neil's friend, Trey was drowning. I wondered if this was one of those moments when time is of the essence when one needs to act, not think, and call 911 ASAP.

Fortunately, I didn't. As it turned out, Trey had picked up my call from the middle of the Raritan Canal where he was kayaking while attempting to balance his iPhone at the same time.

In one of his vocal bursts, I picked up that he was running a bit late for our call and would call me back in a few minutes once he was on dry land. I reassured him that I was in no hurry.

Neil had requested Trey to speak with me and share some of his wisdom—the same brand of earthy wisdom that had transformed Neil into a campaholic.

Neil mentioned that he was first introduced to Trey as *'Tango Trey,'* also his public profile on SoundCloud. Trey, with his well-coiffed dreadlocks, was originally from Jamaica. He took pride in being a digital nomad and had spent a fair number of years in South America, especially in Argentina. Hence the name, Tango Trey.

More recently, Neil discovered Trey's enthusiasm for Travel and began to rethink him as *'Travel Trey.'*

Trey called me back in about fifteen minutes and apologized. He was back on land as was his kayak, both safely out of the water. I was relieved.

"Hi again, Kai. Properly, this time," he added, smiling. "Sorry, I'm late. I underestimated that current. I usually take my flip-phone for these trips, so I don't feel too miserable if I lose it."

"No worries, Trey. Thanks for making the time for me. I'm glad you're fine. You had me worried there for a second."

Trey laughed, "You sound like my mom. All in a day's kayaking at the Raritan canal."

"Is that where you were? I didn't even know they had kayaking," I exclaimed. "And to think I live pretty close to where the canal goes through."

"Oh, you sure aren't the first person to tell me something like that," Trey said. "And you won't be the last. It always amazes me how unfamiliar most people are with what's in their backyard.

"But hey, I'm not complaining. There's more space for the crazy folks like me," Trey exclaimed. "So, how can I help you?"

"Well, I was pretty impressed with Neil's transformation and how he now loves camping. He suggested I speak with you."

"Ah, Neil the *glamper*," Trey said with a smile.

"That man still needs to learn to pack light. He packs his house with him each time he camps. But yeah, he was interested when I told him that camping was one of my travel escapes, especially during the pandemic."

"One of your escapes?"

"Oh, there's a lot you can do, lockdown or not. But let's chat about all that when we meet in person. As I'd told Neil, I wanted to quickly connect with you to first understand what it was you wanted to chat about. Initially, I thought it was something about music. My bad."

Trey continued, "How about we catch up in person on Saturday? You pick the time and place."

"Sure thing. Let's do 3 p.m. on Saturday, then? I'll find someplace interesting."

After Trey cut the call, I wondered how glad I was to have this initial conversation to clarify things. Me and music? I couldn't play an instrument to save my life.

Trey seemed like a free-spirited guy, and I was sure I could learn from him. I wasn't sure what, though. My recent experiences with Vinci Vin and Manimal Mary had started similarly—as a blank slate. I was fast discovering that a blank slate was better to write on.

I started racking my brain on where I would meet Trey. It would be an excellent opportunity to see some places I'd meant to check out myself. I also realized that I wanted to impress Trey with my choice of location. A friend had once told me how she pre-judged people based on the restaurants they chose to meet and how they treated the wait-staff there. The way she put it, our interactions with places and people were reflections of our true selves.

I first thought about golf. Trey and I could go golfing and walk and talk. Only, I didn't know if Trey even golfed and didn't want to ask. He didn't strike me as the type. I briefly considered axe-throwing, but the thought of looking over my shoulder for an axe on an errant trajectory didn't dovetail nicely with easy conversation.

Finally, after much deliberation, I decided on catching up at the local Whitewater mall. The mall had been extensively renovated during the lockdown and its interiors had transformed to resemble a tropical rainforest—artificial streams, canned bird sounds, and fake foliage. In effect, the works. Inspired by Jewel, the architectural rainforest marvel at Singapore's Changi airport, the folks at Whitewater had even created a fifty-foot waterfall that ran from the third floor to the first. It went right into the middle of the food court, where flow dampeners ensured that not a single drop splashed onto people's choice of carbohydrates.

Considering Trey's obvious love for the water, this would be perfect.

The Whitewater mall was true to its name, I learned on Saturday. I'd reached early to grab a good table at the recently opened *Coffee shop by the falls*.

The water cascaded majestically from two floors above, and frothed and foamed at the bottom like the foam on my cappuccino.

Trey had texted me to let me know he was outside, struggling to find a parking spot. Judging by the crowds inside, Whitewater falls indeed was popular. I was glad I'd come early.

"Hey," I heard a familiar voice exclaim from behind me.

"Good to see you again, Trey," I said, getting up.

"Sit, sit. I'll grab a drink and join you."

Fortunately, the queue for the barista was pretty short. I watched as Trey stood in line. He stood out, not only because of his dreadlocks and athletic appearance but because Trey was the only person in the line who wasn't glued to his phone while waiting. He was absorbing the environment and the people around him.

"Where's your drink?" I asked as Trey came back empty-handed.

"Oh, they're brewing a fresh batch of their dark roast and said they'd bring it to our table."

"Isn't that an impressive feat of engineering?" I asked, nodding in the direction of the water.

"It is interesting," Trey agreed. He was still taking in the place—the packed food court with eleven outlets, and the people around the base of the falls taking up-angle selfies to capture the height of the falls behind them. Kids squealed with delight as the mist touched their curious faces when the water dissipated its potential energy through the mesh filters at the bottom of the falls.

"Yow. Waddup."

Trey and I turned towards the greeting to see a young man with a thousand-watt smile. And a cup of coffee.

"One dark roast, and nothing else, just like you asked, brother," he said, handing the cup to Trey, who was also smiling.

"Thenk yuh. How yuh stay?" Trey asked, taking his coffee.

I watched, fascinated as Trey and the man spoke in what sounded like English, but wasn't. I caught intermittent words that I understood. It was almost like some version of *Pig-Latin* we'd use as kids to speak in code. After a few minutes of animated conversation topped with a fist-bump, Trey turned back towards me.

"Sorry about that. That guy was thrilled as was I to meet someone from Jamaica."

"No problem. What's that language you were speaking? It sounded like English though it wasn't exactly English?"

Trey nodded, "Everyone who visits Jamaica gets fascinated by it. And confused."

"I do hope to visit Jamaica sometime."

"Then you should learn some Jamaican Patois. That's the language we were speaking. It's an English based Creole language with strong West African influences, and most Jamaicans speak it. Patois developed in the seventeenth century when slaves from West and Central Africa learned and nativized the English spoken by the slaveholders."

"Wow. I did not know that."

"Yeah, it has its origins in slavery. Interestingly, the language is also heavily used for musical purposes. If you like reggae or dancehall, you have Patois to thank. If you do plan to visit Jamaica, learn some Patois first. With its English roots, it's pretty easy."

"In fact," Trey continued, "this applies to any country or city we visit. It's a great idea to soak in the place's language, culture, and history beforehand. That way, the trip starts even before you get on a plane, and when you finally get there, you're less of a stranger in a strange land."

I was nodding in agreement. It made sense and was in stark contrast to travelers who preferred to find or replicate their native cuisine, language, and community wherever they went.

"Speaking of places," Trey said, interrupting my thoughts, "would you mind if we headed outside. It's beautiful weather, and I should have told you that I sometimes get claustrophobic in malls. Also, this place is getting loud for us to have a good conversation. And hey, if it's waterfalls you like, we're only fifteen minutes from the trailhead for Hemlock falls. Have you ever seen it?"

"No, I haven't," I said, disguising my disappointment with Trey not being too thrilled with my choice of place.

But, I was also curious. The last time I'd heard the word hemlock in a sentence was when poison was involved in a Shakespearean play that I was forced to read in school.

"Let's go, then. You'll like it, I promise," Trey said while typing on his phone.

"There. I sent you a Google Maps link for the parking lot at the trailhead. Let's drive there. Trust me. You'll love it."

We grabbed our coffees and headed out as I took a last look at Whitewater mall falls. A mother was running towards her child, who was precariously balanced at the edge of the base with some newfound friends. Trey was right. It was getting very crowded.

We encountered a young man handing out Vitamin-D samples at the mall on our way out. I took one. Trey politely declined.

"We'll get plenty of that where we're going," he said, smiling.

Trey had parked and was out of his car when I pulled into the *Tulip Springs* parking lot, the closest patch of asphalt to Hemlock Falls. Some people were tossing a frisbee at the grass patch next to the lot.

"You're wearing boots," Trey exclaimed. "Looks like you came prepared for hiking, eh?"

"Oh, these boots have never been on a hike," I sheepishly admitted.

"No kidding. So, what do you use for hiking then?"

"Errr. I don't. Hike, I mean. I do walk outside in my neighborhood, but that's it."

"Oh, wow. This is your lucky day, then," Trey said, with his thumbs up, as we walked towards what was labeled the *Lenape trail.*

"There are so many amazing trails here. You're going to put those shoes to good use."

Trey led the way as we chatted about life, music, and friends. We crossed other groups of people, who seemed to be regulars. It almost felt like I had stumbled upon a subculture within the woods of New Jersey.

We turned around a corner along a red-earth path, the smell of rain from the morning still fresh on it. Trey suddenly jumped ahead of me and turned around to face me and block my way. Extending his hand for dramatic effect, he said, "Allow me to introduce you to Hemlock Falls."

Rounding a corner, I stood, transfixed to the spot, my gaze on the beautiful waterfall in front of me. A couple of kids and their dog were wading in the pool at the bottom as their parents kept a watchful eye at the edge of the water. Towards the top of the falls, it seemed to flow in stages, and people were lazing at different patches of flat rock, looking peaceful and content and getting their Vitamin-D.

I watched it in awe.

"You like?"

"I love it. This place is literally in my backyard."

"You'll be surprised how much we all have in our backyards. We're so caught up with traveling far and wide that we forget to travel *near and narrow*."

"*Travel near and narrow*. That's an interesting expression," I said. "And so true. I've circumnavigated the roads around this place over a hundred times, but I had no clue that places like this even existed."

"Now you know," Trey said, nudging me towards a path of stone steps that rose along the side of the falls. "C'mon, it's a great view from up there, too."

"Circumnavigation," Trey said, dialing back to my comment. "That's not a word people use often. That's interesting."

"Why's that?"

"Ever heard of the *Circumnavigators Club*?"

I hadn't.

"The club," Trey said, "is for people who'd circumnavigated the globe. Its purpose is to encourage fellowship and understanding. It believes that people should see and absorb as much as possible about the world, and it provides a forum for its members to exchange ideas and travel tips."

"That sounds pretty cool," I said. "That must be a magical experience. How do people join?"

"Interestingly, the magician, Harry Houdini, was one of the earliest members. So was at least one US president. The club was founded over a hundred years ago at a time when global travel was especially difficult and expensive. Not surprisingly, early members were famous or rich."

"So, you need to travel to all seven continents to be a member?" I asked, fascinated.

"Oh, no. There are approximately fifty members who have set foot on every continent. But the club has over seven hundred members. To become a member of the club you must travel around the world at least once crossing every meridian of longitude in the same direction, not necessarily in a single trip."

"Let me guess. You're a member?"

"Almost am. I had a few meridians left which I should complete on a trip to New Zealand next month.

I'm usually not a fan of clubs. I subscribe to what Groucho Marx said that he refused to join any club that would have him as a member."

"That's hilarious. But this is not your regular, snooty club, I assume?"

"I've heard it isn't. Members have circumnavigated the globe by balloon, spaceship, sailboat, ship, motorcycle, bicycle, planes, and of course, on foot. They view *Travel* as a way to inform themselves and to have some fun in the process."

"I'm sure you'll fit right in," I commented while trying to keep pace with Trey as we reached the top of Hemlock Falls.

It was even more beautiful from above and to see the water cascading down. Pockets of people were drinking in the view, huddled together at different patches of dry land along the sides of the Falls' path.

We were both quiet for a while, soaking in the atmosphere. Trey took a photograph on his phone.

"So, you said you usually take your flip-phone when you go kayaking?" I asked, interrupting the silence. "How do you take photos, then?"

"I don't," Trey replied.

"I've been here over a dozen times, but this is only the second time I've taken a photo. The way I see it, I can capture an image in my mind or on my phone.

And anyway, we rarely revisit our old photos. Most of the time, they dilute a moment when we could have absorbed so much more if we'd left our phone in our pocket."

"I'm sure the social networks don't like your tribe," I chuckled.

Trey smiled, "Have you seen the documentary, *Happy*?"

"It's on my list. I keep hearing about it," I admitted.

"So, spoiler alert then. Do watch it, though. One of the contributors to happiness is being in a steady state of flow like the water we see here. Travel helps with being in a flow state also known as being in the zone. It's the mental state in which you're doing an activity, and in a feeling of energized focus, full involvement, and joy in the activity."

"How so?" I asked.

"What's the last non-English speaking country you visited?"

"Italy. Almost a year ago, though."

"That's fine," Trey said. "Remember the moment you landed with the anticipation of a new adventure ahead despite the jet lag? You had to figure the way to immigration and interpret signs in a foreign language. You had to find your transport from the airport, figure where to get a coffee or a drink, learn how to ask for it, request directions to places, shop, eat, and buy tickets. All the things that you did were things you would do without thinking back home. They all required renewed focus and thought because you were in a foreign country."

He continued, "Travel reminds us to be in the moment. Even if you went to a new city where everyone spoke English, you'd still need to spend some time reorienting yourself and absorbing the place. That temporary unfamiliarity is one of the best things about Travel. For some people, it is, unfortunately, a stressor."

"I've seen that." I nodded.

"Yup. And just to clarify," Trey continued with a faraway look, "you don't need to travel far to find flow."

"Travel near and narrow," I chimed in. "Like we did today?"

"Exactly. Traveling far requires time. And money."

"And time is money," I added, helpfully.

"It's not," Trey said, with a wink in his voice.

"You have something, contrarian, to say on the subject, it seems?"

Trey was looking around the ground near us, searching for something as he continued, "the expression, time is money, is at best, a cliché. It is useful to think of the two as independent, at least, as far as *Travel* goes."

He finally found what he was looking for—a thin branch to use as a stick to write on the ground, as he squatted down.

"And the reason for thinking of them as independent," he continued, "is because they are the two axes of how you can think about Travel.

"There's the *Time* axis with *Near* at one end and *Far* on the other, depending on how long it takes to get to a place," he said, drawing a horizontal line.

"And the *Money* axis, with *Cheap* on one end and *Expensive* on the other," Trey said, drawing a vertical axis with dollar signs to represent money.

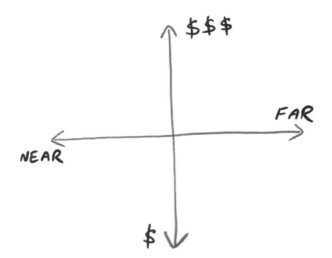

"Now, let's start filling it in. Where would you put that trip to Italy?" Trey asked.

"There, I guess," I said, pointing at the top-right quadrant.

"And how about our hike here today?"

I thought for a while before answering, "The bottom-left?"

"That's right. Near and cheap. And I wonder why people say go take a hike," Trey remarked as he wrote onto the ground.

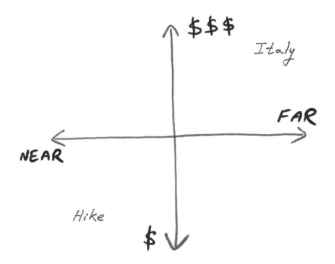

"Now for the not-so-obvious part," Trey smiled. "What would you say goes into the near but expensive corner? It doesn't take time to get there, but it sure needs money."

"Hiking in designer sneakers?"

Trey smiled, "That would qualify, but no."

I thought some more before saying, "A staycation at a fancy hotel, perhaps?"

Trey nodded his head encouragingly. "That works. Lots of people did that during the lockdown for a change of scenery. Anything else?"

"I'm thinking. Wait. What about flying? I mean, locally? A friend once took me flying in a single-engine plane. It's not exactly cheap, and the tiny airport we flew from was fifteen minutes away. Does that count?"

"Absolutely does. I also like it that you're now thinking in the third dimension- vertically," Trey said, nudging me to go on.

"OK, that's a hint then. So, scuba diving would count as well. Again, an hour's drive away, it won't break the bank, but it's not exactly cheap. I still remember what a cousin who's into diving once said. *Same planet, different world.*"

"Now we're talking," Trey exclaimed. "Let me map these out. Flying goes a little higher than scuba since it costs more. And the nearest dive site is an hour away, but the airport is fifteen minutes away. So diving moves a bit to the right of flying. And staycations, somewhere between the two. Agreed?"

I was nodding my head furiously as I added, "I can think of other options for the top-right and bottom-left corners. May I?"

"Sure. Go for it," Trey encouraged, giving me the stick.

I scribbled with the stick as I thought aloud, "Neighborhood or local walks go in the bottom-left. They're even cheaper since there's no fuel burnt to get there. And domestic Travel goes to the top right although it's cheaper and faster than getting to Italy. It could even be a drive to, say, Montreal. It takes more time but less money."

The ground beneath our feet now looked like this:

"Good thinking," Trey remarked. "We've only got one lonely corner. What do you think goes there? It's a tricky one for sure since going far is usually expensive."

I thought for some time, and finally, my eyes lit up, "Going in an RV? You can get far, and it isn't too expensive since you don't have to spend on hotels and can cook your meals."

"Totally agree. Van life has been all in the news in recent months for a good reason. Before we add that in, can you think of anything else—something that involves traveling very far. Much, much farther than even Italy, but interestingly, much, much cheaper."

"Is that even possible? I have a feeling this is one of your riddles."

"Let me give you a hint. Can you travel without moving?" Trey asked with a sly smile.

"If that's supposed to help me, it's not. Hmm. Not time travel, I reckon. Travel without moving. Let's see."

I refused to give up and was lost in thought while looking around. I could hear birds chirping and a bird-watcher looking for the source of bird-sounds through her binoculars in the distance. Some kids were spinning flat stones onto a pool of water, trying to make them bounce off the surface.

Wait. Bird-watcher. Binoculars, I thought to myself.

"*Astronomy*," I shouted, like Archimedes shouting *Eureka* when he was in his bathtub and discovered the principle now named after him. Mary and I had recently discussed it in our conversation about *Bed, Bath, and Beyond*. The memory of that was still fresh.

"Very impressive," Trey said, nodding his head with genuine appreciation.

"I didn't expect you to get that, I'll admit." He continued, "Invest in a good telescope and roam the universe for free. It is *Travel*. Travel that reminds us of our insignificance on this planet. Perhaps, that's the reason why many astronauts are very humble people."

Thrilled with myself, I added, "I agree. I even got that same sense of insignificance when my friend took me flying. From only two-thousand feet above, I struggled to pinpoint my own house—the place that held my all-important self. It was an interesting lesson in humility to remember how small we all are in the grand scheme of things."

"Exactly," Trey nodded. "And you take it a few notches higher when you remind yourself that our planet is small in the grander scheme of things. A Newtonian reflector telescope and a clear night can be great teachers."

"Now, you can fill the bottom-right corner."

I did, and the *Time isn't Money grid* was finally complete.

We started walking back down to the base of the falls when Trey said, "Now, do you see what I meant by traveling near and narrow? What I meant was everyone usually thinks about traveling far and wide—the top-right part. Traveling near and narrow is my way of telling folks that there are many other options."

"Three other corners as you showed me," I said, nodding.

"Exactly," Trey said. "For example, our friend Neil first explored the top-left with glamping—readymade tents with mattresses at manicured campsites. Once he learns to camp even more frugally, he'll move to the bottom-left by camping in the truest sense of the word."

"I do want to clarify that I'm not discouraging traveling to far off places. In fact, I strongly encourage it. As I mentioned, I'm even trying to make it into the Circumnavigators Club," he added.

"I'm only saying that there are many other possibilities. If you are traveling far away, do some homework, and learn about the language, food, history, and culture of the place you visit. Try and travel to the kinds of places you haven't been to. Most folks in the Northern hemisphere, for instance, have never been to a country in the Southern hemisphere."

"Me, for one," I said.

Trey and I were chatting away, and before we knew it, we were back at the Tulip Springs parking lot. On the way back, he shared how there was no shortage of variety and explained to me that each hiking trail had eight versions.

Doing a route in reverse would provide a different look and feel from walking in the other direction. He said that the same trail would look, feel, smell, and sound different in summer, fall, winter, and spring.

Trey was curious about my name as he'd met men and women named Kai across the world. I told him my name meant *the sea* or *ocean* in Hawaiian. It also meant *ocean* or *recovery* in Japanese, *victory* in Chinese, *food* in Maori, *rejoice* in Swedish, and *the willow tree* in Navajo. He observed that I had a name perfectly suited for traveling as I thanked him for his time and thoughts.

"Let me show you something cool," he said as he opened the trunk of his car. Inside was a holy mess of all things outdoor, including a beautiful grey and orange Celestron telescope.

"For my bottom-right corner," he smiled.

"Nice. I also noticed the foam mat there. Are you into yoga?"

"I am, and coming to think of it, have I ever seen you at Mary's class? When we first met, I thought your face looked familiar."

"Ah, yes. I was there recently to learn from Mary. Not yoga, but life. And on a day not unlike today."

"Now, you're the one speaking in riddles. But yeah, Mary's cool. I'll tell her we met," Trey added as he hugged me goodbye.

I waved as he pulled off from the lot, new-age jazz music playing from his open windows. I'd decided to sit at a grassy knoll nearby to watch the sunset.

It was one of those evenings when the sun and the moon were simultaneously visible like two playful balls in the sky. The moon glowed in reflected glory as the sun bathed the sky in a fiery shade of burnt-orange before she stepped away to bestow a glorious new day to other parts of the world. It would soon be morning in places, far and wide.

I was still traveling. Traveling near and narrow.

* * *

"The three most harmful addictions are heroin, carbohydrates, and a monthly salary."

— Nassim Nicholas Taleb

CHAPTER 7

Name

Joe's friend Cora introduced herself to me via email, with a cryptic, two-word subject: *Hyperbolic Reflectors*. This, I learned in the body of the email, was the name of an exercise she wanted me to do before we were to meet on Sunday at a strange address of her choosing. I would soon learn that shock was par for the course as far as Cora's conversations were concerned. Very clearly, she found wicked delight in it, even if she hid it well behind a stoic expression.

Having been introduced to astronomy by Trey, I knew a bit about reflectors and refractors in telescopes. I wondered if Cora was also into star-gazing. Even if she was, what did reflectors have to do with our meeting?

Cora's email had stark but clear instructions:

Hello Kai,

I'd like you to paste the following text today to your Facebook profile, verbatim, please:

Friends, I need a favor that should take a minute of your time. I'd like you to imagine that you meet someone who you think might know me. To find out if they do, you start to describe me to that person. What sentence(s) would you use in this scenario to describe me as you begin with,

"Do you know Kai…"

Please DON"T answer in the comments below. I'd like this to be anonymous so that you can be honest. I'm an adult. Can take it:)

Please enter your answers at http://bit.ly/HReflect

———

I'll explain more when we meet.

Regards,

Cora

When I first met Cora on Sunday, she struck me as someone who had little appetite for pleasantries and small-talk.

"What do you think humans have in common with seahorses?" she asked me, less than five minutes into our conversation, with what I'd best describe as a classic poker face.

A month ago, I would have been taken aback by a question like that. But Cora's email earlier in the week and my conversations with Vin, Mary, and Trey over the last three weeks had dulled the part of my brain that reacted negatively to surprises.

I was grateful for that.

Of course, there was also the fact that thanks to Mary, I was now acclimatized to being asked '*spot the difference*' questions between humans and other species. It was also becoming a recurring theme these days.

It was evident that Cora wasn't your "typical client." I was surprised that Joe was very comfortable asking his client to spend time with me, a total stranger.

Not wanting to jeopardize his relationship with his client, I asked him if he was OK doing so. He reassured me that Cora, who wore many hats through her chequered career, was happy to speak to friends of friends. And especially about abandoning classic career paths. *Careerless-Cora* he called her, only half in jest.

And careerless, she was. I had gone through her LinkedIn profile earlier and was impressed and confused.

I was impressed by the many senior positions she'd held, her education, the professional societies she was a part of, and her online essays. She had won many awards and was associated with more than three non-profits across the span of thirty-five years of work experience.

I was confused by my inability to connect dots and see connective tissue between the different roles and firms where she'd worked. They were sparsely correlated and almost seemed, well, unexpected.

Equally unexpected was the venue for our meeting. We were at the *Liberty Corner Fire Company*, a volunteer fire company where Cora was finishing up with cleaning *Squad 40*.

Every alternate Sunday morning was cleaning day. Various volunteers were busy with their tasks. There was a palpable camaraderie in the air—the type that comes from a shared purpose and mission and from the inimitable joy of committing to the service of others. There was also an air of unspoken efficiency.

The place was spotless as was Squad 40, the department's newest fire truck, a 2019 *Pierce Enforcer pumper* with a two-thousand gallon per minute pump. As Cora put it, that was like pouring four-hundred large buckets of water every minute. *Almost a mini waterfall*, Trey might have said.

"Dancing?" I thought for a bit before answering Cora's question on seahorses.

"I didn't know seahorses could dance," Cora said with an amused smile. "So, even if that's correct, it was not the answer I was looking for."

I thought for some more time before finally shrugging my shoulders and giving up.

"They pair-bond like most humans," Cora said with the smile of a quiz-master allowed to divulge an answer after all teams had passed.

"Pair-bond? What does that mean?"

"It means they're loyal to a mate for the time they are together. Few species do that. Most species are, in fact, polyamorous, where it is typical for the male or female of the species to have more than one mate at the same time. Elephants, tigers, deer, apes, bees, spiders, too many to name are all polyamorous."

"I didn't know that. I've only heard of the black-widow spider where the female eats her mate. That's creepy. Reminds me of that one hit song by Space, *The female of the species is more deadly than the male*."

We both laughed as Cora clarified, "I haven't heard the song, but that line was first said by Rudyard Kipling, who's most famous, of course, for writing *Jungle Book*."

"So, about your question, did you ask me about seahorses to bring up pair bonding?"

"Ah, yes. I wanted to highlight that pair bonding was the exception and not the rule, and that humans take it to giddy limits."

"How so?" I asked.

I half-expected a sermon on free love and societal impositions. With her spontaneous laughter, the bright red highlights in her wavy hair, and oversized bamboo earrings, Cora did strike me as someone who might have grown up through Woodstock and the Flower Power movement. She was probably a teenager then, though, I mentally calculated.

"Don't get me wrong," Cora said, interrupting my mental math. "While I think it's a free world and each person has the right to do what works for them, I'm personally all for pair bonding in relationships. But, we ought to stop at relationships."

She continued after a pause, "Most people pair-bond with their work."

"Pair-bond with work?"

"Yup. It's like the expression where we say someone is married to their job. It's not usually an exaggeration. But what I mean by pair-bonding at work is not about being a workaholic. It's something deeper."

She took a moment to think before continuing, "Take Joe, for instance. Let's pretend I don't know Joe at all, which is, of course, difficult to believe considering he introduced us to each other. But, play along with me here. If we met a year ago, how would you have described Joe to me?"

"Hmm, how would I describe Joe?" I muttered to myself, my sixth sense feeling a connection between Cora's question and the hyperbolic reflector exercise she had asked me to do.

"It helps to start with saying *Do you know Joe? He's...*" Cora trailed off, emulating a wave with her hands to explain her point.

"All right. I'll try," I said, clearing my throat.

"Do you know Joe? He's a management consultant at Deloitte. He focuses on supply chain management. Earlier, he used to be in the M&A advisory team, but he does less of that now."

"That was good," Cora said encouragingly.

"Now, let's come back to today and assume I still don't know Joe. How would you describe him?"

Having now gotten the flow of things, I expected to hit the ground running. Surprisingly, it took me some time to compose my thoughts.

After thinking a bit, I said, "Do you know Joe? Or, Dr. Joe as some of us call him. Great guy to have at parties as he's a certified Emergency Medical Technician. That's his volunteer gig. In his day job, he's a management consultant."

"Super. Now, I want you to imagine you're me. Which Joe do you think I would be more interested in meeting? Last-year-Joe or Today-Joe?"

"Today-Joe," I answered without hesitation.

"Why's that?"

"Today-Joe sounds more interesting. More interested in helping society for sure."

"Would you say, then, that Last-year-Joe was relatively uni-dimensional?" Cora prodded.

I nodded in agreement.

"Why did you take a longer time to describe Today-Joe?" she asked.

"I guess because he's multi-dimensional. More colorful. I had to pick and choose which part of his life to lead with and hence thought about it a bit more."

"Exactly! And that's a great lens right there. If your friends struggle to describe you to their friends, that's great. It means there are more dimensions to you, and that people need to choose their descriptors."

"So, that's one part of it," Cora continued. "The second part is about you. Do you realize that in both cases, Last-year-Joe and Today-Joe, you chose to describe his job?"

Cora was right.

She added, "I assume that's how you answer when someone asks you the question: So, what do you do? Answer with details about your job? Is that right?"

"I do," I replied with a guilty voice.

"Don't worry about it," Cora said encouragingly. "So do ninety-nine percent of all people. Everyone assumes their titles, and the names they hold in organizations define them as people. And that's the unfortunate reason that the same people who complain about never having the time to stop and smell the flowers get the jitters when they're laid off or when they're between jobs."

"Overnight," she continued, "they lose their sense of identity since it is anchored to a job or an occupation. They behave as if they got divorced instead of being 'funemployed' even when they can afford the break. Makes sense?"

I agreed. I could relate to this, having felt the same each time someone asked me, "So, what do you do?"

I would reply with the details of my job and responsibilities. Perhaps, add a sprinkling of where I live and my family, almost as an afterthought.

I remembered hearing from a South-African friend that he had a group of friends whose ice-breaker question wasn't "So, what do you do?" Instead, it was, "So, what do you play?" In a country with a demonstrated penchant for sport, the sport one played or associated with was a defining part of their personality.

"It's all about color," Cora said, interrupting my thoughts. "It's first about expanding the color palettes of our lives. That's what helps us describe ourselves and others when asked what we do. And that's a good segue into your hyperbolic reflector."

It felt like Cora was reading my mind. "I was wondering what happened with that. What's with the name, though?"

"Oh, it's a play on words. When people talk about their friends, they tend to indulge in hyperbole. They exaggerate parts of their personality that they think stand out, similar to a caricature artist. And someone else speaking about you is, in effect, a reflection of your personality and character traits. Hence, the name, hyperbolic reflector."

"That's interesting. So, do tell me, what did my friends say about me?"

"I don't blame you for being curious. I'll let you read the answers later. So, here's what I did. I used an online program that takes all the responses people gave and creates a word cloud highlighting the most common words. Here's yours."

Cora had taken a screenshot of the word-cloud on her phone. She cherry-picked words as she eyeballed them along with me.

"As you can see, most of it is about your profession and career."

"Oh," I said, unable to conceal my disappointment.

"Helpful and cheerful come a few times too. You're fun at parties and are a person people know they can rely on. And, I caught a few interesting words that weren't too frequent but stood out."

"Like what?"

"Papercraft, outdoors, and a few others."

"Ah," I smiled. "That might be due to my interests in Origami and hiking. Recently, I've been posting pictures of things I make and links to trails I hike."

"That's interesting, and I'm glad you have new interests. You see, work experience is overrated," Cora continued. "Some people say they have twenty years' experience, when, in reality, they only have one year's experience, repeated twenty times."

"Ouch. But, I can say I've seen that," I said.

"I can't take credit for it," Cora admitted. "Stephen Covey said that. It's bang-on. Imagine the epitaph of, say, an accountant who chose not to add color to his life. Here lies Luis, amazing father, husband and friend, and excel virtuoso par excellence."

"You've got an interesting sense of humor," I smiled.

"Yeah, my friends have gotten used to what they call my amusingly morbid side. Hopefully, you'll get used to it too."

"Oh, I've had plenty of practice," I added. "I have a dear friend, Raj, who teaches at Oxford—part of a close group of friends. Raj has a fascination with the obituaries. We have a WhatsApp group where every once in a while, he forwards something interesting, more often than not, it's an obituary."

"I'd like your friend, Raj," Cora said, "I recall reading that if you want to know of man's accomplishments, read the newspaper starting at the obituaries. If you want to learn of man's failures and pettiness, start with the front page."

"That's sad but so true," I said, nodding. "Recently, Raj forwarded us an obituary of this amazing person, Michael Hawley, who unfortunately died of cancer sometime during the pandemic. He was a computer programmer, professor, musician, speechwriter, and helped lay the intellectual groundwork for what we now know as the Internet of Things."

"That's very impressive," Cora agreed.

"There's more," I continued. "He wrote commencement speeches for both Larry Page of Google, and Steve Jobs."

"How's that for a life well-led?" Cora said with genuine amazement. "We can't all be Michael Hawleys, but his life is a fantastic example of adding color to life. Of expanding our palette. See how many sentences you needed to describe him. Each of us has stories to tell, and the more colorful, the better. It also helps with making up better stories."

"Making up stories?" I asked, squinting my eyes.

"Yeah. I learned that one from my brother. He's an Issac Asimov fan who quotes Asimov's laws for robots on every available occasion. As though he didn't have enough on his plate already, he recently started writing a science fiction book. He keeps saying that it is important for an author to inhabit many worlds. And that the only way this is possible is by expanding your horizons and having many interests. That way, you can create a fictional world at the intersection of, say, bread-making, rap music, and paragliding, or any unique intersection that creates a new context and background. In effect, a new world."

"That makes a ton of sense. In retrospect, I can see a lot of authors' interests spilling into their work. So, dialing back to what you mentioned earlier, how does one add color to their palette?"

"It's not as difficult as one might think. It simply starts with thinking nine to ten instead of nine to five."

One more riddle, I smiled to myself as I reflexively asked, "Nine to ten?"

"Yes, we're all conditioned to think nine to five, the typical working hours for a workday. We're trained to focus on career paths. But, it's better to think of life one hour at a time, instead of one workday at a time. That way, you'll do more activities at work and outside of it. Otherwise, you run the risk of being that person with one year's experience, repeated many times."

"And how does one figure what those activities are? I mean, how does one add that color you mentioned? For the nine to tens? Is there a formula to it?"

"If there is, I don't know it," Cora said. "But I do have some ideas. Have you ever heard of the Japanese concept of Ikigai?"

"No, I haven't."

"It means the reason for being—your reason for getting up in the morning. The idea of purpose and reasons for being are nothing new, and they have been explored and dissected in various cultures. Recently, Ikigai has become quite popular, partly because it has a very visual representation that is easy to understand and appreciate. Let me draw it out and show you."

I accompanied Cora as we walked from the engine parking bay into the firehouse training room, where they had a whiteboard that the firepersons used during training. After a brief search for working marker pens, Cora started to draw out what seemed like an elaborate Venn diagram. When completed, it was powerfully simple.

"There are four key areas here as Marc Winn first illustrated," she said as she drew four perfect circles on the whiteboard. "What you love, what you're good at, what you can be paid for, and what the world needs."

"The theory goes," she continued, "that true fulfilment and happiness, and some say a long life too, can be found at the convergence of these four circles. And that, in the smallest nutshell, is Ikigai."

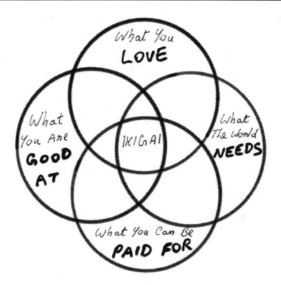

"If one of these is missing," Cora continued, "you get the feeling something's off. It could be a sense of financial insecurity or a sense of uncertainty if you're doing something you're not good at. Or a sense of emptiness if, hand to heart, you don't love what you do."

I jumped in, "Or of not being useful when what you do isn't what the world needs. This is what Joe said he felt during the pandemic, and one of the reasons he did that E.M.T. course you pointed him towards."

"Exactly," Cora agreed, "though I must confess that all I did was introduce Joe to a friend at the *Liberty Corner First Aid Squad*, another volunteer organization in town. I often find that to know about something new, *Who* beats *How*."

"*Who* beats *How*? What does that mean?" I asked.

"It's simple, and I'll keep it brief as I don't want to derail our Ikigai here. If you want to explore something new, it's always better to speak with someone *Who* knows about it rather than try and learn *How* over the internet."

I nodded in agreement. That was precisely what I'd done with Vin, Mary, Trey, and now, Cora, who had returned to the whiteboard. She was filling out the pros and cons of each group of three intersecting circles.

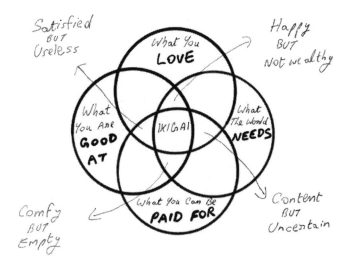

"Everyone is trying to find that perfect center. It's elusive, and thus, it pays to aim for a combination of things around the edges."

I added, "You make it sound like a dartboard. Aim for the board first before trying to hit the center."

Cora nodded appreciatively, "That's a lovely analogy that I'm going to borrow. And our friend, Joe, is a perfect example of aiming for the edges."

"How so?"

"Well, Joe's not good at being an E.M.T. Not yet, at least, considering he just started. Joe's certainly not doing it for the money since he's pretty comfortable financially. Joe's doing it because he loves medicine, or used to, at least. And because the world needed it."

"Yeah," I agreed. "He's like a man on a mission nowadays."

"Mission's the perfect word," Cora said, writing it at the intersection of two circles. She proceeded to fill the other intersections—'petals' as she called them. She wrote the words, passion, profession, and vocation.

She stepped back from the board and stood alongside me as I let it all sink in. It was a lot to absorb, but it made a lot of sense.

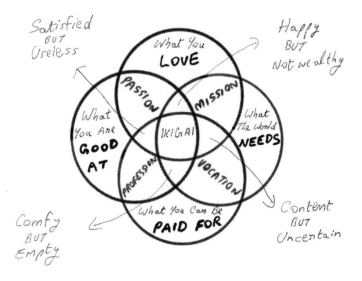

I took a photograph of the whiteboard as Cora had brought out the eraser and said she'd be erasing the board.

"Putting it very plainly, we usually focus on one of these four dimensions," Cora said as she erased most of the diagram except for the last four words she'd written.

"*Profession* is our typical answer to the *So, what do you do* question. We should be adding *vocations, passions,* and a *mission* to that mix. Ideally, a mission that helps others. That's it. Life isn't that complicated, you know."

"Not when you put it the way you did," I agreed. "So, how do I cultivate the seeds for these?"

"Good question. Hector Garcia and Francesc Miralles, in their book on Ikigai, talk about ten rules that can help people find their Ikigai. I can't remember all the ten, but they're pretty commonsensical. Stay active and curious, stay in shape, and a state of flow, reconnect with nature, surround yourself with good people. Those kinds of things."

"*Names, Places, Animals, Things,*" I said, involuntarily.

"What's that?" Cora asked.

"I just realized something," I said, smiling. "Something connected. In the last few weeks, I met some fascinating people. Like you, they were generous with their time and wisdom. Between them, they taught me a lot about what you just said—curiosity, flow, nature, and staying in shape."

"Oh, OK, that's interesting," Cora said, very matter-of-factly. I sensed she wasn't comfortable being labeled a fascinating, generous, and wise person though she knew she was one.

It was getting late, and I wanted Cora to have the rest of her weekend to herself. I could also see the firehouse winding down as others were locking up and leaving for home. Cora excused herself as she went to check something with her colleagues.

While waiting, I took another photo of the whiteboard. It was another digital memory of an insightful and life-changing Sunday. I thought about my transformative conversations over the last few weeks with Vin, Mary, and Trey. And now this chat with Cora that seemed to bring it all together. I owed a debt of gratitude to my friends and our conversation at Gina and Neil's *mask burning party*.

It was amazing how everything is connected as are we. And if we only bother to seek those connections, there were connections in names, places, animals, and things.

I was lost in thought when Cora came back in and smiled as if she was reading my mind. She cleaned the whiteboard before I could offer to do it and walked out with me. I thanked her for everything.

On our way out, we passed the well-appointed firehouse gym. One of the perks of being a volunteer fire-person, Cora explained.

I noticed a couple of yoga mats in the corner. "Don't tell me you're into yoga too?" I asked Cora.

"Oh, not me. Not a chance," Cora clarified. "A few folks at the station are, though. And it's catching on. Even my brother recently got into it. I'm glad since it gets him outdoors."

She continued, "He's usually at home or tinkering in his garage. Now, every Sunday, he's at the park doing his downward dogs, and even helping his instructor with building an app for her classes."

"Is this the same brother who's writing that sci-fi book?" I asked.

"Yup. He's the one. Vin's a geek. He has more wires around his head than hair on it."

* * *

"I have no special talents. I am only passionately **curious**."

— *Albert Einstein*

"**Humility** is not thinking less of yourself, it's thinking of yourself less"

— *Rick Warren*

"**Empathy** is the ability to step outside of your own bubble and into the bubbles of other people."

— *C. Joybell C.*

CHAPTER 8

Rebirth

"Go around. Go around now," I muttered to myself.

A *Piper Cherokee* on its landing leg seemed suspended in the air as it floated towards the runway. It was descending a lot slower than the pilot intended. From its glide-path, I could estimate that it would, at best, touchdown after having wasted over half of the available runway. Given the little remaining runway to come to a full stop, this could be dangerous. It was the textbook definition of a situation that demanded a 'go-around.' Not something that is seen often enough in aviation, go-arounds require a pilot to abort a landing, apply full power and take off to come back again and attempt a better landing.

The pilot of the Cherokee, like many new and experienced pilots, was hesitating. As she hesitated, the seconds to a possible disaster were counting down.

Almost as if on cue, the air was punctuated by the sound of the Cherokee's engines urgently roaring back to life as the pilot applied full power. From its position twenty feet above the runway, the plane began to climb slowly. Within a minute, she was back at pattern altitude and ready to re-enter the downwind leg to try another landing. Hopefully, a better one, this time around.

I briefly inhabited the world of aviation when I took a couple of flying lessons, thanks to Trey's point on the vertical exploration of new places. I was intently watching the Piper Cherokee as silence hung in the air between the four of us. It was the kind of silence that accompanies the moment when you are abruptly transported back to the 'here and now.' Especially after a long and engaging story when you are unsure how to continue where you left off if you even remember where you left off.

Raj, as he often did, broke the stalemate, "That explains a bunch of things, Kai. It explains how you've been up to so many things, and why you've generally been incommunicado at times."

"Sorry, if I have," I said. "Sometimes, I did tend to get rather immersed in what I was up to."

"Wow. Just, Wow," Mona said. "That's some story."

"And thanks for sharing it," John added. "Gives me a ton of hope for sure."

"Gives us all hope for our respective midlife crises," Mona smiled. "So, what happened after that? Between then and now? Tell us more."

The winds seemed to be changing direction, and a gust almost blew away the napkins I'd spread out across our table. I'd used them to illustrate and share some of the lessons I had learned—lessons about names, places, animals, and things.

"As you might remember from college, I'm a visual learner. I had all these fantastic lessons from Vin, Mary, Trey, and Cora, which I shared in my story and these napkins. Somehow, I felt the need to connect the four lessons before going ahead and acting on them. Almost like beads on a necklace. And so, I did."

"I have a feeling that this is about that work of art on your phone," said Raj. "The stick figure you shared earlier?"

"You're right, Raj. It is," I admitted as I pulled out a pen and reached for another napkin.

"At the rate at which you're going, I wouldn't fault the restaurant for charging us extra for napkins," Mona remarked.

"This is the last one, I promise."

I sketched out a simple person as a child would.

"That's a brilliant replica of Leonardo Da Vinci's Vitruvian man. I can't tell the difference," Raj remarked with a deadpan expression, as the others joined in, laughing.

"Yeah, when's your art exhibition?" John added.

"Laugh all you will," I smiled, joining in the good-natured banter.

"But there's golden wisdom in this picture. And Raj, interesting that you mentioned the Vitruvian man. The less well-read among us call it the Renaissance Man. And what I will soon be showing you is a playbook for a personal renaissance. For anyone. You'll see."

"Ignore these jokers. Boys will be boys," Mona said. "So, what's the significance of this?"

"I'm glad there's an adult among you. Let's go with the order in which I shared my story. Thing, Animal, Place, Name. Fair warning, I'm going to quiz you to find out how much you listened."

"For once, I'll be at the receiving end of a quiz," Raj said, suddenly interested.

I started with my questions, "So, what do we use to make and do things?"

"Our hands," Mona instinctively replied.

"Absolutely. So, each hand represents a *thing* you're thinking of making or doing. Two hands, two things. Just write them in. For now, I'll write in *Thing 1* and *Thing 2*. My first two things, by the way, were, not surprisingly, Origami and the Arduino."

"And how often would you change your *thing*," John asked?

"That's a very, very relevant question. Change it too often, and you'll be flitting from one thing to the other before you even have a chance to figure it out and know if you enjoy it. Changing it too infrequently is a recipe for boredom. I did it both ways before figuring what I believe is the perfect cadence. I do it every quarter as Vin recommended."

"Almost like the seasons," Mona remarked.

"Absolutely. Almost in sync with the four seasons, I revisit my NPAT, as I like to call it, every quarter. Like clockwork, four times a year, I've diligently done it eight times over the last two years. I even have a reminder on my calendar for it. By the way, I follow this quarterly cadence for *Name*, *Place*, and

Animal too. We'll come to those in a minute. Any questions?"

"Yeah, how do you even decide on the things you might want to make and do?" Raj asked.

Before I could answer, John chimed in, "The *Physical Fertilizer Model?* Map out things as *physical* or *virtual* on one axis, and on the other, based on knowledge. It depends on whether you have a lot, some, or no prior knowledge. *NPK* as Vin called it."

"Perfect," I said, clapping my hands.

John added, "And once you have a bunch of things, use that to populate your *calendar of curiosities*. Every quarter, as you recommended."

"You're bang-on again, John," I said, turning to Raj. "Now, we know who's not been listening."

"Okay, okay," Raj raised his hands in mock surrender as he asked, "so, can we do four *things* instead of two? I mean, you have an upper arm and a lower arm, after all?"

"You could," I said. "I'll admit, it is tempting when you have many things down on your NPK grid. I suggest you do more than two things only if you have the time. Considering everything else we're juggling in life, I would suggest picking two for starters. And look, if you're not challenged enough, by all means, increase it in the next quarter."

"Of course, you being you, Raj, you'll probably do more. And, as a professor, you also have more free time than the rest of us," Mona dug in, good-naturedly.

Raj was always competitive and liked to over-extend himself. It was a recurring theme and a source of much ribbing from the rest of us.

"What about the other parts? *Animal*, *Place*, and *Name*?" Raj asked, eager to change the topic.

"We'll talk about *Name* later. Let's move on to *Animal* first. Do you remember what Mary shared?"

"I loved the three-balls analogy," Mona answered. "I could relate to it at so many levels right from the word juggling itself. And she's right. We do prioritize that financial ball made of steel over the relationships one made of porcelain. The most important one that many of us ignore till we're on a bunch of pills or have a wake-up call of sorts is the one on health. That one is made of glass."

"Yes, that's a great analogy to remember to focus on health over everything else. If you're not alive and healthy, nothing else matters. What else do you remember?"

"I remember the six-pack mnemonic," John said. "Body on top, Brain at the bottom, thanks to the gut-sy joke, pun intended. And Breath connecting the two. BBB, as Mary called it."

"And the two-word guidance?" I asked, encouraging him to go on.

"Go slow," John correctly remembered.

"And BBB can also be *Bed, Bath and Beyond* for creative inspiration," Mona added. "As did Kekule, Archimedes, and Newton."

I agreed, "Yup, they were all going slow when they made their world-changing discoveries. Kekule was in bed, Archimedes in his bath, and Newton was beyond—under an apple tree."

"An apple tree in Cambridge where Newton was sheltering when the bubonic plague was going around," Raj added. "It's almost a shrine of sorts, especially to physicists. It's even called Newton's apple tree."

"That's very interesting," I agreed, getting back to the napkin sketch of my renaissance person.

I thought aloud, "Let's put the Body, Breath, Brain six-pack in the most obvious place for it. And, moving on to places. We go places with…"

"Our legs!" Mona shouted before I could complete my sentence.

"Absolutely," I agreed. "So, in our little picture, as you did with the hands for things, you write out, on the legs, two places you intend to explore this quarter. And yes, you can do four too. Follow the same logic that we talked about a little while ago. Let's go over Trey's recommendations on travel once again."

"*Time isn't money*," Raj answered. "I couldn't agree more with that statement, by the way. I always thought the common expression, *time is money*, forced a commercial lens on our existence."

"You're so right about that, Raj," John said, adding, "so, map out places on the time and money axis, and pick a couple of new ones every quarter, I guess. Sounds very similar to what we did with the physical fertilizer model for things."

"It is. What else do you all remember from what Trey said?" I asked.

"Travel near and narrow," Mona answered.

"And far and cheap," John added. "Like, Astronomy. That's a big one on my bucket list by the way. I'm wondering now why I put it away all these years. I'm writing that onto my left leg right away."

"Nice kickstart to your NPAT and renaissance man," I said, encouragingly.

"And, do you need to change your stuff every quarter?" John asked, still super-focused.

"Look at John. The star pupil with all the great answers and questions," Raj interjected before I could respond.

"He is," I agreed. "It's best to review your NPAT every quarter. As I said, I do mine on the first day of each calendar quarter and have a reminder on my calendar until eternity. I go over everything on my list of possibilities—*Things* to make and do, *places* to go, and ways I plan to connect with my inner *Animal*. And yes, some introspection on the *names* and titles I carry too. We'll come to those in a bit."

"Do you remove what you had in the previous quarter?" John queried.

"Not necessarily. There are three possibilities if you think about it," I said, counting off my fingers.

"First, you tried something before that didn't resonate with you as much as you expected. If you're sure you don't want to do it anymore, remove it. Make space for something new in a new quarter. For example, for me, that was flying. It ticked off my *things* and *places* lists simultaneously. But, a few classes in, I decided it wasn't for me. I still enjoy watching planes as you may have guessed from my choice of venue today," I said.

"So," I continued, "even though I didn't pursue it, I briefly inhabited the world of aviation. I discovered places like this and met colorful, differently-wired people. I'm richer from that experience. In short, everything adds up even if you drop it from the list. That's the beauty of trying new stuff."

"The second possibility," I counted off, "is one where you tried something, enjoyed it, and want to continue to do it. Perhaps, even make it a regular practice. For me, funnily enough, and despite my initial reluctance, that was Yoga. I finally caught that bug when it appeared in my NPAT for a couple of quarters. After that, it became a habit and dropped off my NPAT. Once in a while, it comes back in when I want to do a deeper exploration, for example, try a new style of Yoga."

"And the third possibility," I continued, "is that you tried something and may do it sporadically, but it's not new to you anymore. For example, I finally succumbed to Jasmine's pitch on sensory deprivation tanks and had that in my *Animal* list for a quarter. I tried it a couple of times, and still float on occasion, but it's not new anymore. So, it's off my NPAT. You could say it is a non-daily habit."

"It was like Origami was for me," I added. "After a quarter of rediscovering my childhood love for it, I immersed myself in paper folding all kinds of species and objects for a quarter. I still fold paper for my friends' kids or to help me be in the moment. I have three apps on Origami on my phone and am richer from what I did that quarter. But no, it was not on my NPAT anymore. In short, my NPAT every quarter is for what I want to try out or explore deeper that quarter."

"Isn't there a fourth possibility?" Mona asked.

"What's that?" I asked, curious about what I'd missed.

Mona, always the one with a keen eye for detail, said, "What if you had something on your list, but couldn't give it the time or attention it needed. So, you don't know if you liked it or not. Shouldn't you keep it on the list for the next quarter as well? To give it a fair chance?"

"Excellent point. I totally agree, and yes, that happens, because, well, life happens. In those cases, you should take an honest look at it at your quarterly review and decide if you want to park it for now or put it down for the next quarter. Sometimes, you have no choice but to park it. For example, learning to snowboard on the local slopes was on my list of *Places* once. It didn't happen, and putting it down for the next quarter's NPAT was not an option since it would soon be spring. So, it hibernated till the next winter. And by the way, it was great fun. I even have my own snowboard now. Once I knew I loved it and that it would fall into my annual habits bucket, it made sense to buy one rather than keep renting."

It was beginning to get dark as dusk flirted with the horizon. The fireflies were already out, flashing signals to potential mates, possible bright spots in their two-year lifespan. In the distance, as if to remind us of Cora, we heard the siren of a fire-engine. Hopefully, it was not rushing for anything serious—perhaps someone who didn't replace their smoke alarm batteries in time.

"That leaves *Name*," Mona said, articulating everyone's thoughts.

"Interestingly," I remarked, "there isn't much to do in this department.

"Doing things, getting in touch with ourselves, going places, thinking nine to ten instead of nine to five, are all portals to new experiences. You'll end up discovering new vocations, passions, and hopefully, missions, too," I paraphrased.

"The *Ikigai petals*," John correctly remembered once again. He was the star pupil.

"Exactly. Those four intersections were profession, passion, vocation, and mission. Playing in those sandpits can be fun. While some of them will be things you choose not to pursue, others will become a part of you—a part of how people describe you. More importantly, how you describe yourself."

"*The Hyperbolic Reflector*," Raj recalled.

"I knew that would appeal to you," I smiled. "Yes, indeed. My reflector was quite an eye-opener for me when Cora shared it with me."

"I'd love a copy of that text that Cora asked you to post on Facebook," Raj said. "I think I'll do the same thing. I'm curious about how people describe me."

"Sure. I'll email it to you. Only, don't ask your students to fill it out. They'll use it to vent any pent-up frustration."

Everyone joined in the laughter as I added, "Just one suggestion on *Name*. Cora and Joe didn't mention it, but as a firewoman and an EMT, they lived it themselves. Don't forget the *mission* petal. It is important that each of us, at some time in our life, hopefully, sooner rather than later, does something regularly in society's service. In effect, it's at the intersection between what you love and what the world needs. For Joe, it was the intersection of his love for biology and the desperate need for frontline workers during the pandemic."

"Totally," Mona said, vigorously nodding in agreement.

She was always socially conscious and had, ever since I'd known her, carved out time in her calendar to volunteer for something or the other. During the pandemic, she was a regular volunteer at her local food bank, helping pack much-needed supplies into cardboard cartons on an assembly line dotted with other volunteers.

She added, "By the way, I've watched that documentary you mentioned—*Happy*. Interestingly, besides flow, the service of others is cited as a key source of happiness."

John nodded, "That's a great point, Mona. Don't just do it for others, do it for yourself too."

As we were speaking, I had filled out the rest of my NPAT renaissance person.

"Speaking of doing stuff for oneself," John interrupted, standing up. "I need to go to the men's room. So, please pause the conversation. I don't want to miss anything."

"It's almost dusk," I said. "We should be heading back anyway and before any mosquitoes arrive. I'll ask for the check. And yes, we'll wait for you, John. Don't worry, I'm pretty much done, anyway, with my stories."

John walked with a perceptible bounce in his step. It was evident that he was energized and had a renewed sense of purpose.

"Kai," Raj exclaimed in a loud whisper. "We should head out. I've been getting a ton of texts asking when we're coming back."

Despite John's protests, we had planned a small surprise party at my house. I was glad he'd be in an excellent mood for it—a far cry from how he was a couple of hours ago. Mona and Raj echoed their relief that John was in a much better space than he'd been earlier.

"Let's leave the moment he's back. And once we reach home, you folks go ahead. I have something to hold him back while you prepare the others for the surprise," I said, reaching out for the check as the waiter brought it.

A flurry of animated competition accompanied an argument on who would pay it. We still hadn't gotten used to the typical approach of splitting the check. A *tetra* meet-up would usually involve the host picking up most of the tab. This time around, that would be me. But, Raj beat me to it.

"Allow me," he said, "I'm used to being on the giving side of wisdom, so this evening is a welcome change. And I'll deny saying this later, but, wow, that was some story, Kai, and those were some useful life-lessons."

"Amen," Mona echoed. She added with a wistful smile, "Isn't it interesting how we've grown? Around twenty-five years ago, we'd each be doing our best acting in ignoring the check when it came, hoping someone else would pick it up. How much has changed, eh?"

"What's changed, and what did I miss?" John asked.

"Nothing much," I answered. "Just that we used to fight to avoid paying the check a few decades ago, and now we're fighting to pay it. You didn't miss much, except for seeing that pilot who did a go-around. She came back for a textbook perfect landing."

"Neat," John said, adding as we walked back to my car, "You know, I realized something when I was in the bathroom. I have no clue what Vin, Mary, Trey, or Cora do for a living."

Mona nodded, adding, "Isn't that amazing in itself? Of course, we know that Mary is a yoga teacher, but that's on the weekends. And Cora's a firefighter, but that's her voluntary role, not her day job."

I agreed, "I now know what they do for what we typically and unfortunately call a *living*. I didn't, at that time, and you're right. Their *professions* are inconsequential to the story I shared with you."

"And yet, it's our first line of defense when someone asks what we do," Raj observed.

"The first line of defense is a great way of putting it," Mona agreed.

"We measure our self-worth by our titles, as Cora mentioned."

We started the drive back in silence, each of us lost in our thoughts. My friends' lives had changed this evening. They knew it, and so did I. I was glad I could help them just as I'd been helped not too long ago.

"You know," John said, interrupting our conversations with ourselves.

"This whole Name, Place, Animal, Thing approach is a recipe for becoming irresistible."

"Now, that sounds like a mid-life crisis if I've seen one," Mona laughed. "What do you mean, irresistible, John?"

"I recall reading this article about the three keys to becoming irresistible. It mentioned that all interesting people had *curiosity*, *humility*, and *empathy*."

"I'd vote on those three too," Raj chimed in.

"But, how do you see that connected to NPAT?"

"Well, I think we can all agree that NPAT is a formula to fuel curiosity. Curiosity enables you to partake of the buffet of experiences that life has to offer. The more you explore, learn, and know, the more you know what you don't know. So, it cultivates a sense of humility."

"That's so true," Raj agreed. "Reminds me of the anti-library."

"What's that?" I asked.

"It's something that the philosopher and writer, Umberto Eco, spoke about. He had a gargantuan personal library containing thirty-thousand books.

There's even a YouTube video that shows him taking a never-ending walk through it. He admits he hasn't read most of them but adds that books we read are far less valuable than the ones we don't."

"Wait, did I hear that right? Books that are read are less valuable?" I asked.

"It's counter-intuitive, right?" Raj agreed. "In Umberto Eco's view, the library should contain as much of what you do not know as your financial means allow. Unread books are a reminder of how much more there is to know. He calls this collection of unread books an anti-library."

"That's so beautiful. It captures what I feel each time I'm in a real library," John acknowledged, as he continued his earlier stream of thought.

"A diet rich in curiosity and humility," John said, "as the anti-library reminds us, is a prerequisite to developing empathy. It helps cultivate an appreciation for differences, and refines our ability to walk in the shoes of others."

"That makes sense," I agreed. "You reminded me of a talk by Jon Meacham, a Pulitzer Prize winner. He said that great leaders must have exactly those same three traits—curiosity, humility, and empathy. He went on to give great examples of how great presidents had demonstrated these virtues."

"It reminded me about what Cora told you about stories and inhabiting many worlds," Raj observed.

"And stories remain our best way of building empathy," Mona added.

"That's deep, Mona," Raj exclaimed.

"I wish I could take credit for it," Mona said, as I pulled into my driveway.

"It's something one of my favorite authors said. I forget which one though. I'll blame it on the margaritas."

"Speaking of forgetting," I said, giving Raj and Mona a knowing wink. "John, before I forget, and since you said you were keen on astronomy, I wanted to show you the Celestron telescope I have in my trunk."

"I've seen enough telescopes on campus. I'll go ahead," Raj said, catching the hint about John's surprise party.

"Me too," Mona echoed.

I opened the boot, where there were two things neatly nested. A case that looked very much like a wheeled trolley-bag that would qualify as cabin baggage. The other was a thin, cylindrical tube, about two feet long. I opened the 'trolley-bag' to reveal a red LED flashlight, paper sheets, marker pens, and a beautiful, bright orange telescope.

"It's a catadioptric telescope," I explained. "Telescopes are usually refracting or reflecting. This one combines the best of both technologies."

"Wow," John exclaimed, running his hands over the contours of the *Celestron NexStar*. "Can we check it out?"

"We sure can. Not tonight, though. It's too cloudy. And hey, it's your birthday, remember? While I didn't get you a gift, I'd like you to have that," I said, pointing at the tube next to the telescope.

"What's that? Your old telescope?"

"No, it's got a *poster* rolled-up inside. Open it. Take a look," I encouraged.

"Don't tell me you got me a poster of one of my favorite actresses for old times' sake," he laughed, as he reached for the poster-tube.

"I wouldn't scandalize you in front of your family," I said, as we recalled the many pin-up posters that adorned John's dorm room in college.

"This one's been my guide for some time now, and I'd like you to have it," I said, as John took the poster out and unrolled it.

"I never expected us to have the conversation that we did today," I admitted. "But, since we did, this poster will now make sense to you. I've used it to constantly remind me about names, places, animals, and things.

Thanks to a recent exploration into sketching and illustration, I created this some months ago."

Twilight and the light from the car's boot illuminated the poster as John held it between his hands.

"Wow. Wow. This is amazing. It brings it all together," John said. "Are you sure, though, about me having it?"

"Oh, I'll make myself another one. With one little edit, thanks to you."

"Thanks to me? What edit is that?"

"I'll show you," I said, reaching into the telescope's trolley-bag for a marker pen.

I drew a triangle on the Poster as John continued to hold it outstretched, curious about what I was doing.

"Like Superman's logo," I explained, as I wrote three letters with the marker. I wrote them unto the three sides of the triangle: C H E. Short for *Curiosity, Humility, Empathy.*

"Now, it's truly yours. Your NPAT. Happy birthday, old friend."

WWW.NPAT.LIFE   #NPAT

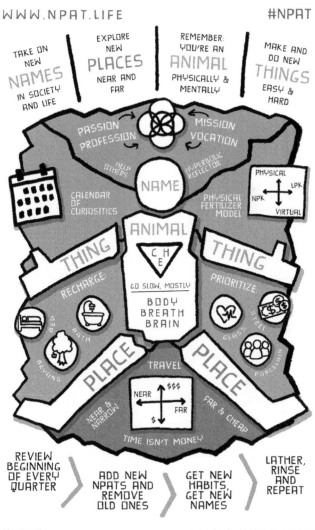

* * *

"Stories remain our best way of building empathy."

— Khalid Husseini

Afterword: Your NPAT

Life is about doing foolish things.

That's what I reminded myself as I embarked on the journey of writing this book for you. The ideas presented here have been in my head for many years, and I wrote earlier drafts of this book in planes, trains, automobiles, and between work. But, I wasn't thrilled with the idea of asking you to read it, until now.

At some point in my writing journey, I decided to gut-renovate this book. I'd made the cardinal mistake of reading one's work before it is finished, and I'm glad I did. The earlier tone, classic non-fiction advice book, was not something I would have enjoyed. So, it felt unfair to ask you to do the same.

As a result, I decided to rewrite it as the "modern fable" you just read.

Considering my fascination with storytelling and a long-time love affair with the fable format, this seemed the best way. Other books that have inspired me in this genre include *Jonathan Livingston Seagull*, *The Monk Who Sold His Ferrari*, *The One Minute Manager*, *The Alchemist*, *The Go-Giver*, *The Café on the Edge of the World*, and *Who Moved My Cheese*.

So, thank you, dear reader, for making it all the way here. I hope you enjoyed reading this fable as much as I did, writing it.

I've never written a fiction or non-fiction book before this. Attempting a marriage of the two styles as a debut effort seemed rather foolhardy.

Did it work? I'll never know unless you tell me. Please do so by reviewing this book on Amazon or sharing your opinion at the book's website, NPAT.life

All feedback is welcome. It will only help—like a hyperbolic reflector.

NPAT.life has many other resources, some of which appear in the fable. A few, in no particular order, are as follows:

➤ A free hi-res download of the poster John got from Kai—in full color

➤ Free templates of the renaissance person to fill in and use

➤ The Hyperbolic Reflector in all its glory

➤ A useful collection of links on Names, Places, Animals, and Things

> ➢ A free newsletter on NPAT, twice a month
> ➢ The NPAT podcast.

They will help you with something I encourage—your renaissance.

Here's the TLDR version of NPAT:

Make and do new things, easy and hard.

Remember, you're an animal, physically and mentally.

Explore new places, near and far.

Take on new names, in society and life.

Create your NPAT plan today. You only need this book, a sheet of paper, a pen, and primitive drawing skills. And some quiet time to think, reflect, and write.

Use John's poster as a guide to remind you of the process of figuring your *things, animals, places*, and finally, *names*.

Or, use a renaissance person template from NPAT. life if you're not in the mood for drawing or are mysteriously deprived of paper and pen.

Either way, please start now. And lather, rinse, and repeat every three months. The world needs it from you.

More NPATs translate into more stories.

More stories translate into more empathy.

The world needs more empathy.

I can't wait to hear about your adventures. If you write about them on social media, please use #NPAT in your posts. That way, we can learn from and be inspired by each other.

Want more NPAT in your life? Try the biweekly newsletter at NPAT.life for starters. I painstakingly and lovingly write every single one, and it's my primary method of staying in touch with friends like you.

Stay curious. Stay humble. Stay empathic.

Namaste!

LuxNarayan.com

www.NPAT.life

* * *

"Good friends, good books, and a sleepy conscience: this is the ideal life."

— Mark Twain

"So, I love you because the entire universe conspired to help me find you."

— Paulo Coelho, The Alchemist

Acknowledgments

"*Omwana taba womoi*," or as we say in English, "It takes a village."

I've often wondered why movie credits are so long. Now, after taking stock of all the people I want to thank for this book, I wonder how they're so short. In an attempt at some semblance of order, I'd like to thank three categories of people:

- People who've helped me in life
- People who've helped explicitly with the book
- People who have no idea I exist but have influenced this book

Like the Ikigai diagrams, there are overlaps between these three buckets of generosity.

In the first bucket, I must first thank my family for providing the canvas for the experiences that funneled into this book. My parents encouraged curiosity, and

I was fortunate for that. My mom, Malathi Narayan, also read an early draft of this book. My dad, A.L. Narayan, who first introduced me to this genre typified by the likes of *Jonathan Livingston Seagull*, would have diligently redlined it and then shouted from the rooftops about it if he were around. My wife, Tina, is my bouncing board for all endeavors in my adult life. Her detailed feedback on early drafts was invaluable, as is everything else she does. Our sons, Shaan and Arya, read early drafts and provided candid feedback of the helpful kind. They also flagged some inconsistencies I totally missed and reluctantly blessed the dad-jokes in the book. I continue to learn a lot from them.

Other family members who provided inputs on early drafts of the book are my sister, Parvathi Narayan, Vikram Ravi (who created the first NPAT after me), and Rakesh Kunhiraman. I'm also grateful to my uncle, S. Narayanan, who introduced me to *The One Minute Manager* and other books and ideas when I was a student. My late grandfather, A.N. Ramanathan, was my partner-in-crime for many childhood adventures. I'm also grateful to my extended family, the Hypers, and especially the Lyngdohs. Through the lockdown, their upbeat spirits made us feel like we were vicariously living life at Lyngdoh Cottage in Shillong.

Friendship is a recurring theme in the book. It anchors the entire narrative, as it does my own life. I am blessed with and grateful for many good friends.

The book saw no less than five iterations thanks to very insightful feedback from my generous friends. Sundar Ramaswami and Kalpana Sundar (also my Mary aka Yoga teacher) provided the best first round of feedback I could have asked for. I am grateful for detailed inputs from Karthik Nagarajan, Peter Claridge, Mary Ann Koruth, Ramki Muthukrishnan (great suggestions on Tetra and Newton), and Jyotika Menon. I had at least one uncomfortable (for them) conversation with each of them where they pointed something(s) that didn't work, and I'm glad they did. It certainly made for a better book.

People who influenced characters in the book include dear multi-avatar friends like M.V. Bhaskar and Ram Gupta, who inspired the *Hyperbolic Reflector*. Other character influences include Naresh Sabharwal, who introduced our family to the Himalayas, and Ken Thai, the handiest man I know. For the aviation theme that runs through, I have the lovely people at my flight school at Somerset Airport to thank, especially my teachers, Byron Hamby and Jon Hanlon. For the book's title, I have my childhood friends from the Indian High School, Dubai, to thank for many paper sheets on which we played Name, Place, Animal, Thing.

For providing the confidence to write this book in the first place, I am grateful to Anant Rangaswami and Yashraj Akashi. They may not even remember this, but they were among the first to hear the ideas behind NPAT many years ago and encourage me to build on it. These two gentlemen were also instrumental towards my talk on "Lessons From 2000 Obituaries" at TEDxGateway and thereafter, thanks to a serendipitous meeting with the multi-faceted Juliet Blake, at TED's New York HQ. I must also thank the best Unconference I have ever attended, WPP Stream. The concept behind NPAT was first born at Stream Jaipur during a three-minute presentation called "Ignite Talks." Thanks also to Dan Martell of SaaS Academy, who, among other things, reminded me of the incredible power of visual models. My startup journey at Unmetric, the company I co-founded, provided the canvas for these experiences. For this, I'm grateful to my amazing colleagues, clients, and investors like Nexus Venture Partners, who I am fortunate to count as friends.

I wrote this book in 2020 through the pandemic and am genuinely grateful to the frontline workers who helped us all stay safe and alive through it and afforded us the luxury to do mundane things like write books.

I'm also thankful to many WhatsApp groups that helped buffer the isolation—IIMC PGP 30, Pineapple Express, IITM Narmada 93, Chennai IIMC—you know who you are. NPAT's newsletter subscribers and friends like Meena Mahajan provided great feedback. Some of the concepts here were first shared with them and then massaged into the book. Writing a book is a physically demanding process, especially when you're doing it at the rate of three-hundred words a day. Saravanan and the committed health coaches at Amura.ai helped me shed thirty pounds and dial up my health and energy levels during my book-writing phase.

In 2020, I binged on many classes and experiences, which provided vital scaffolding and helped with writing. I must thank David Perell and his exceptional *Write of Passage* class for refining my online writing habit and catalyzing the birth of the NPAT newsletter. I am also glad for connections that sprung from it—my writing buddies, Gwyn Wansbrough, Shirish Pai, and Jennifer Vermet, and my writing coaches, Ellen Fishbein and William Jaworski. For a break from writing and the clarity that distance affords, I owe a huge debt of gratitude to Dhamma Dhara in Massachusetts, where I spent ten disconnected days in absolute silence while learning the beautiful practice of Vipassana meditation. Starting this on the day after I finished the first draft of my manuscript lent some much-needed distance from the book and the opportunity for introspection. The other notable source of 'relief' was Improvolution's Improv drop-ins and shows, the Comedy Cellar's live-streamed comedy on Mint Comedy, and my weekly Freestyle Hip-Hop sessions with the Messy Philosophers and David "BS" Bradshaw. Thanks to all the funny people in my life. Laughter is indeed the best medicine.

I have many people to thank for manifesting the process from ideas in my head to the lines you are now reading. Scribe Media taught me the writing process with their excellent (and free) resources and book, and my patient coach, Emily Gindlesparger, who read the first outline of this book (very different from now), guided me on the writing process for this genre. The creative Paul Hawkins designed the cover and the poster at the end of the book. I met Paul through Reedsy, who has the most comprehensive collection of resources for authors. Besides resource matching, the free content on their website and blog is liquid-gold for writers. The best UX designer I know, Amrinder Sandhu, helped with inputs on the line drawings and his opinions on all other things design related. The hard-working team at Notion Press managed the proofreading, editing, layout, and production of the book (thanks to Navin, Vandana, Surekha, Chetna, Sarvesh, and Mithila). Chandler Bolt's *Self Publishing School* helped ease me into the otherwise complicated world of book marketing, and I am glad for the inputs I've gotten from my book launch coach, Ramy Vance. I am also grateful to Sreenath Reddy and his team at Intentwise for their expert inputs on Amazon marketing. I should also add the very articulate online classes and content by Dave Chesson of Kindlepreneur as something I am grateful for. Cutting Edge Studio and their founder, J.Sharpe (also an author) helped in many ways, including creating a trailer for the book. While on the subject of marketing, I serendipitously attended a boot camp on PR by Chris Winfield and Jen Gottlieb of Superconnector Media. Among other things, it was a masterclass on running a boot camp. I hope to work more with them in the future.

On to the last bucket: People who mostly have no idea I exist but have influenced ideas in this book.

Starting with *Places*, there's the Sunset Pub and Grill at Lincoln Park, New Jersey. Yes, it is as beautiful as it sounds. The book's other *location credits* go to the Circumnavigators Club, the AllTrails app for Hemlock Falls and many other trails, and the Liberty Corner Fire Company in Basking Ridge, NJ. Then, there's Tentrr, whose glamping sites provide people with some much-needed breaks, even more so during the pandemic when outdoor was the only way to go. For places down under, I have Temple Adventures in Pondicherry to thank, especially Rob Partridge, Aravind Tharunsri, and Neela Bhaskar, for reigniting my love for scuba diving. *Same planet, different world.*

HGTV's Flea Market Flip inspired my wife, Tina, to make me the lovely writing table featured in the book and upon which I wrote the book. Lastly, on *Places* and in keeping with the bottom-right quadrant, thank you, Celestron, for your excellent telescopes and for delivering us a NexStar 6E during the pandemic. It opened our eyes to the skies above and helped us travel far and wide without moving. Thanks also to the United Astronomy Clubs of New Jersey (UACNJ) for keeping virtual activities going through the lockdowns. Their website's footer says it beautifully: This site is powered by the universe.

For the ideas behind *Animal,* I have to thank Andy Puddicombe and Headspace for first getting me hooked on meditation many years ago. Then, there's Andy, Ryan, Jarlo, and the fantastic team at GMB.io who, in my opinion, run the best and simplest whole-body fitness program there is, especially with their focus on movement and their overall approach to the body. For sensory deprivation, thanks to Joe Rogan in whose podcast I first heard about the tanks and to Quantum Floats' well-maintained facility in Bedminster, NJ, where I experienced it.

James Patterson and Malcolm Gladwell's Masterclass classes on writing were more than worth the entire subscription to the Masterclass platform. I devotedly consumed them over many drives and hikes. Further on inspiration, *The New York Times* Obituaries team (@NYTObits on Twitter) writes the most inspiring section of their paper. The founder of 5-Hour Energy, Manoj Bhargava's thoughts on useful and entertaining things, was a driver towards this book's format. On curiosity, humility, and empathy, I am inspired by the work of the historian and presidential biographer, John Meacham. I have also been inspired by John Gorman's writing on Medium. As Raj says in the book, and as I mentioned in my TED talk, there's something about the name *John*.

Almost lastly, I'd like to thank Nymeria, aka Nim, our dog. Yes, I did observe her. And yes, it was weird.

Finally, a day before this manuscript goes into the *locked mode*, I'd like to thank all the people who read my NPAT newsletter and kindly agreed to read advance reader copies of this book. Thank you, Brian Condon, Venkateshwarulu aka Dijjer, Deepika Mahajan, Hari Sury, Natarajan Gautam, Anthony Hendrickson,

Vandana Vaidyanathan, Ravin Kurian, Shirish Pai, Sanjay Mehta, Anurag Dwivedi, my cousins, Subha and Uma Narayanan, Diana J. Scott, Suresh Pradeep, Sandeep Achantani, Shankar Hari, Manish Agarwal, Gwyn Wansbrough, Jay Rampuria, Sumedh Reddy, T.N. Pratap, Suresh Raju, Martin Daniel, Hemant Nadakuditi, Navin Kalani, Rahul Mehrotra, Ben Noah Suri, and Venkatesh Krishnamoorthy.

Some of my fellow authors also generously agreed to read advance reader (author?) copies of the book. Thanks, Vineet Vijayghosh, Jessica Foley Griesbach, Susan M. Baker, Deidre Stokes, Irial O'Farrell, Brett Preiss, Vanessa Wilcox Thurgood, Susy Lee, Rebecca Ewal, LaDonna Goodman and Mari Ki.

I'm pretty sure that I've missed some folks in the above list and in general. That's the nice thing about web pages. An updated version of the *Acknowledgements* can be found at *https://luxnarayan.com/NPAT-thanks-you*.

Omwana taba womoi, indeed.

* * *

About the Author

Lakshmanan, aka Lux Narayan, is a student of storytelling.

He loves the seas, skies, and mountains and is a scuba diver, pilot, and an avid hiker. His adult sons share his love for adventure. His wife and best friend, Tina, and their dog, a rescue from Hurricane Maria, partake in all ground level adventures.

Lux's talk at TED's Main Stage on "Lessons from two-thousand obituaries" was viewed millions of times, featured on the TED homepage, and NPR's TED radio hour with Guy Raz. He is a student of improv and stand-up comedy and has performed at the Comedy Cellar in New York.

A serial entrepreneur, he founded Unmetric, a social media analytics company that was acquired in 2019. Lux advises a few startups and nonprofits, is an independent board member at a public FinTech company, and in 2021, co-founded WordsWorth.ai

He is forever learning to type with all his fingers. This is his first book.

Lux divides his time between Basking Ridge, New Jersey, and Chennai and Shillong in India. Stay connected with him and his (mis)adventures at LuxNarayan.com and NPAT.life.

* * *

Made in the USA
Middletown, DE
20 February 2021